The British Army 1660–1704

John Tincey • Illustrated by Gerry Embleton

Series editor Martin Windrow

First published in Great Britain in 1994 by Osprey Publishing,
Midland House, West Way, Botley, Oxford OX2 0PH, UK
44-02 23rd St, Suite 219, Long Island City, NY 11101, USA
E-mail: info@ospreypublishing.com

Transferred to digital print on demand 2010

First published 1994
3rd impression 2005

Printed and bound by PrintOnDemand-Worldwide.com, Peterborough, UK

A CIP catalogue record for this book is available from the British Library

ISBN: 978 1 85532 381 0

Series Editor: Martin Windrow
Filmset in Great Britain

Artist's Note

Readers may care to note that the original paintings from which the colour plates in this book were prepared are available
for private sale. All reproduction copyright whatsoever is retained by the Publishers.
For information, please visit www.gerryembleton.com
The Publishers regret that they can enter into no correspondence upon this matter.

Publisher's Note

Readers may wish to study this title in conjunction with the following Osprey publications:

Men-at-Arms 98   *Marlborough's Army 1702–11*
Men-at-Arms 203   *Louis XIV's Army*
Elite 25   *Soldiers of the English Civil War (1): Infantry*
Elite 27   *Soldiers of the English Civil War (2): Cavalry*

FOR A CATALOGUE OF ALL BOOKS PUBLISHED BY OSPREY
MILITARY AND AVIATION PLEASE CONTACT:

Osprey Direct, c/o Random House Distribution Center,
400 Hahn Road, Westminster, MD 21157
Email: uscustomerservice@ospreypublishing.com

Osprey Direct, The Book Service Ltd, Distribution Centre,
Colchester Road, Frating Green, Colchester, Essex, CO7 7DW
E-mail: customerservice@ospreypublishing.com

www.ospreypublishing.com

THE BRITISH ARMY 1660–1704

INTRODUCTION

The period between the Restoration of Charles II in 1660 and Marlborough's decisive victory at Blenheim in 1704 is often seen as something of a 'backwater' of military history. The struggles of the English Civil Wars were over and Marlborough's epic campaigns yet to begin. However, this 40-year pause was far from a period of peace and inactivity. It was marked by the defeat of the Monmouth Rebellion at Sedgemoor in 1685, the 'Glorious Revolution' in 1688, the ambush at Killiecrankie in 1689, and the battle of the Boyne in 1690. Overseas it saw the garrisoning of the British colonies of Virginia and the West Indies; expeditions to Bombay and Portugal; and the defence, against overwhelming odds, of the British bases at Dunkirk and Tangier. The 1690s brought direct involvement in the European power struggle – with large numbers of British troops deployed against the French in Flanders at the pitched battles of Walcourt (1689), Steenkirk (1692) and Landen (1693).

Indeed, the period was vitally important in the development of Britain's armed forces: it saw the birth of the British army in its modern form, and the establishment of many regiments that survive to this day.

Yet it is not a period that can be easily categorised; it spanned the reigns of three monarchs, each with a fundamentally different attitude to the army. Charles II (reigned 1660–85) feared the old Cromwellian army and tried to destroy it before rebuilding an army he could trust.

Detail of an engraving showing the Horse Guards in 1684. Hats rather than pot helmets are worn, as are cross belts for sword and carbine. Cravats are also in evidence. A description by C. C. P. Lawson of the oil painting upon which this print is based says that the soldiers wear 'buffish grey coats'. Unfortunately we know that cavalry at this time wore buffcoats but we also have evidence that they wore grey 'undress' coats. From Windsor Races, 24 August 1684 *by Francis Barlow, 1687. (Private Collection)*

James II (1685–88) lost much of this hard-won trust by trying to lead England back to Catholicism. William III (1688–1702) used the British army largely as an auxiliary force to the highly trained Dutch army in his own wars on the Continent as well as in the British Isles – a difficult but, as it turned out worthwhile apprenticeship. When Marlborough took over command in 1702, the British army knew its trade well enough to take on the armies of the great powers of Europe on equal terms.

To attempt to trace the political and religious struggles, and the many campaigns fought during the reigns of these three monarchs is beyond the scope of this book. Indeed, to write at all of a 'British' army at this time is something of a misnomer – separate armies existed in Scotland, Ireland and England. The main purpose here is to reconstruct the uniforms and equipment of this period. This is not a straightforward task. There was some regulation of uniform, but most details were left to individual regiments. Unfortunately the government 'patterns' – garments approved centrally setting basic standards – were destroyed by fire many years ago. The

Captain Francis Hawley commanded a company of 45 grenadiers of the 1st Foot Guards during an attack on Monmouth's rebels at Philip's Norton in Somerset. He wears a red coat with light blue facings and gold decoration which appears to be based on the regimental uniform. At this time officers' uniforms were beginning to come under some regulation although they were still provided by the officers themselves. Officers continue to have considerable freedom in choosing the quality of cloth and decoration to suit their personal tastes. Hawley is depicted holding a smoking grenade and a match-cord; he has a plug bayonet on his waist belt, suggesting he would have been armed with a fusil in action. Oil painting by an unknown artist, dated 1685. (Private Collection)

Right: A troop of the Horse Guards at Charles II's coronation in 1661. An oil painting of the event shows tiny figures of a troop in buffcoats although an account from some years later observed a troop in short red jackets. The buff-coats or jackets worn by this troop under their back and breast plates have many tabs or skirts, and are decorated with metal or lace strips on the sleeves. From an engraving by Wenceslas Hollar.

uniforms reconstructed here are therefore based upon eyewitness reports, a few paintings and engravings, and bills and accounts for the purchase of uniforms.

For weapons and equipment the situation is slightly better as these were provided through the Ordnance Office and much of the paperwork survives in the Public Record Office in London. The evidence begins with a few documents scattered randomly through the records for the reign of Charles, becomes organised volumes for the reign of James and is an unscalable mountain thereafter. The bibliography lists some of these sources, and also gives details of the books and articles of those who pioneered research in the field in the last century, and of those who currently labour in the archives. Where possible, original quotes have been reproduced in the text, as many of the details for this period remain contentious.

THE ARMY OF CHARLES II

Following the Restoration of Charles II in 1660, Parliament intended to destroy Cromwell's army, and instead rely on scattered garrisons and the militia for internal security and national defence. However, when an uprising by religious fanatics in London routed the militia, regular soldiers had to be brought in to restore order. King Charles was thus provided with an excuse to maintain a force of 'personal Guards'.

The Tangier Garrison

The marriage of Charles II to a Portuguese princess, Catherine of Braganza, brought the colony of Tangier to England as part of her dowry. The port stood on the African Atlantic coast near the straits of Gibraltar and it was hoped that its possession would open up English trade with Africa. Unfortunately the local inhabitants proved to be unfriendly, making the outpost a heavy drain on resources and bringing few benefits. Initially a garrison regiment for Tangier was formed numbering 1000 men in ten companies under Lord Peterborough. Three further regiments were sent from Dunkirk after that town was returned to the French.

In April 1663 the new governor of Tangier, Lord Teviot, strengthened the town defences considerably by constructing a line of blockhouses and trenches on the ring of hills dominating the town. The Moors reacted by staging repeated attacks on the new works. One of the more unfortunate incidents occurred in May 1664 when Teviot with 500 men was lured into an ambush while foraging for wood and building materials. Teviot was cut down and only 30 soldiers escaped. Fortunately the Moors were distracted by internal feuds and the reduced garrison of 1415 foot and 140 horse was able to hold out.

After 1678 the Moors became increasingly hostile and with the aid of European renegades attempted a formal siege of the colony. A section of the defences were overrun with heavy English loss, and many of the surrounding hills became permanently occupied by Moors. Percy Kirke was sent out as the new governor to restore the situation. He brought with him two combined battalions of 600 men each, one drawn from the Guards regiments and the other from Dumbarton's Regiment, so that by October 1681 the garrison numbered 3221 foot and 120 horse. On 27 October 1680 a force of 1500 men comprising six infantry battalions, seven troops of horse (including some hired from Spain) and a naval brigade, marched out to fight the Moors. For once the tribesmen accepted battle face to face and were routed by cavalry charges and musketry, losing some 500 men. But this minor victory was not enough to save the colony: in 1683 the garrison and settlers were shipped back to England.

Other colonies

Charles II's Portuguese marriage also brought England possession of Bombay. In 1661, 400 foot in four companies were sent to take over the colony. The local Portuguese commander, however, was unwilling to give up his post and it was not until November 1666 that the 97 surviving English soldiers took up occupation in the colony. Rather

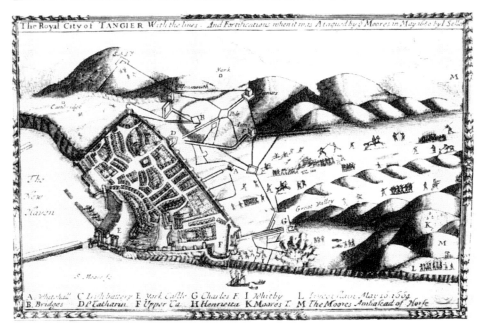

The Royal City of TANGIER With the lines. And Fortifications when it was Ataqued by ye Moores in May 1680 by I. Seller

A Whitehall C Irish battery E York Castle G Charles F. I Whitby L Lower New May 16 1684
B Bridges D Pa Catharine F Upper Ca. H Henrietta K Moores I. M The Moores Ambassad. of Horse

The African port of Tangier became an English possession as a result of Charles II's marriage to the Portuguese princess, Catherine of Braganza. This plan shows the ring of hills which overlooked the town, together with the forts and earthworks constructed to secure them from the Moors. From an engraving dated 1680 by I. Seller. (National Army Museum)

short-sightedly, Charles considered Bombay to be of no long-term value; in 1667 he sold the place to the East India Company for an annual rent of £10.

England also had colonies in the Americas in close competition with the French, Dutch and Spanish. British troops were sent out in response to various threats, but lack of funds meant they generally went unpaid and were the first to be disbanded when the government needed to save money. Jamaica was garrisoned by two companies from 1677 to 1682; Barbados had its own regiment from 1667 to 1671; and New York, recently captured from the Dutch, had in 1667 a garrison of 300 men, of whom none remained under arms by 1679. A rebellion in Virginia in 1676 prompted the emergency shipment of 1000 British troops, though they arrived to find the rebel leader already dead and his supporters defeated.

Foreign expeditions

In addition to colonial service many soldiers found themselves fighting under foreign command as allies of European powers. In 1662 three New Model Army regiments forming the garrison of Scotland were reduced into two regiments each of 1000 men and were shipped with a regiment of 1000 horse to fight under Portuguese command against Spanish invaders; they remained overseas until 1668. Charles II took advantage of this expedition to remove a number of troublesome anti-monarchists in the army from the country.

A British brigade had been in service with the Dutch since the 16th century. In 1665 the outbreak of war with Holland caused the force to be disbanded with many of the

returning soldiers recruited into the Holland Regiment and the Admiral's Regiment. Peace came in 1674 and a new Anglo-Dutch brigade was formed comprising three Scottish, one Irish and two English regiments.

France had long been a favourite destination for British soldiers of fortune, who served mostly in separate British regiments under officers of their own nationality. This tradition came to a temporary end in 1678, when Parliament forced Charles to abandon his French alliance to side with the Dutch. Several regiments including Dumbarton's were made to return from French service. Many veterans found themselves transferred into a new force earmarked as aid for the Dutch, with the Duke of Monmouth (himself just returned from French service) in command; a force of 17 battalions of infantry, 10 squadrons of horse, 9 squadrons of dragoons and 20 guns – 17,860 men in all. However, King Charles was not willing to lose his secret French pension and he managed to repeatedly delay the sailing of the force. The troops did reach Flanders in the end, but only Monmouth with his personal followers was present at the final battle of the war. The men were left to make their way home, disease-ridden, poorly provisioned and, as usual, lacking pay.

Scotland and Ireland

As well as the English army, Scotland and Ireland maintained their own forces, which were independent but still owed their allegiance to King Charles II. In Scotland a regiment of Foot Guards and a troop of the King's Guard of Horse with a few small garrisons brought the total strength of the Scottish army to 1200 men. This army was mostly employed in suppressing the Lowland religious opponents of the government; it rarely ventured into the Highlands. The most serious problem came in 1678 when a force of 6000 Covenanters rose up in rebellion. The Duke of Monmouth was dispatched with one regiment of foot, three troops of horse, a company of dragoons and two groups of Highlanders – some 2754 soldiers in all. The forces met at Bothwell Bridge where Monmouth's regulars swept the Covenanters from the field in a single charge.

Ireland also maintained its own forces, though strict instructions forbade the recruiting of Catholics. At the Restoration the Irish garrison stood at 66 companies of foot and 30 troops of horse. In April 1662 a regiment of Irish Foot Guards was raised, together with 60 'Guards of battleaxes' for ceremonial duties. By 1676 the garrison had been formed into six regiments each of horse and foot. However, pay was always in short supply, and in order to prevent starvation, foot soldiers had to be allowed to work as labourers and horsemen and given leave to return to their own farms.

THE ARMY OF JAMES II

In the enthusiasm surrounding the coronation of a new king, Parliament forgot its long-standing battle over the royal finances and granted James II generous revenues. The celebrations were soon soured when a pretender, the Duke of Monmouth – who as the first-born son of Charles II had a claim to the throne – landed at Lyme Regis in Dorset hoping to raise the West Country in revolt. Five days later he marched into Taunton at the head of 3000 men having routed the county militia and captured many of its weapons.

The initial response to the Monmouth Rebellion was confused as small battalions composed of a number of companies from a regiment were ordered westward. Immediately James set about recruiting new units to bolster the old ones. The force that was finally assembled was made up of a troop of Horse Guards of 150 troopers and 60 Horse Grenadiers, seven troops of the Earl of Oxford's Regiment of Horse, three troops of the Royal Dragoons with another on outpost duty, 13 companies of

The harquebusier armour of James II. The tri-bar face protector here incorporates the Royal Arms of the Lion and Unicorn. Few ordinary soldiers would have been issued with the metal bridle gauntlet. The flexible jointed scales made this an expensive piece of equipment. (Royal Armouries, Tower of London)

QUEEN ♣

The Defeat of the Rebells
2000 Slayn & their Canon taken

Design for a playing card depicting the final phase of the battle of Sedgemoor. Monmouth's rebels are chased off the field leaving behind three cannon and a scythe turned into a weapon by altering the angle of the blade. Though the uniforms are generally correct, the royal soldiers are depicted with out-of-date sword baldricks rather than waist belts; and the flag has a St. George's canton in the style of the Civil War; this design seems to have been replaced in the 1670s with a St. George's cross running across the entire field of the flag. (Private Collection)

the First Foot Guards, six companies of the Coldstreams and five companies each of Dumbarton's, Trelawney's and Kirk's Regiments. With 24 cannon in support the Royal Army numbered some 700 horse and dragoons and 1900 foot. Monmouth at this time commanded an army of 3–4,000 men of whom around 600 were mounted. At Sedgemoor, the Royal Army was surprised by a night attack and only the steadiness of Dumbarton's Scots prevented disaster; but the tide of battle was turned and Monmouth's force was destroyed. Though many of the new regiments had been raised purely to suppress the

rebellion, James II took the opportunity to keep them under arms.

The Glorious Revolution of 1688

During the Sedgemoor campaign the army had remained loyal to King James despite overtures from Monmouth, even though Monmouth had earlier been the army's Captain-general. Only three years later the situation had changed radically. In his attempts to reintroduce Catholicism, James had shown increasing favouritism towards Catholics and had recruited them in preference to Protestant officers in the Irish army. Such policies were not popular in the army or among the public at large.

William of Orange invaded Britain partly for fear that Britain would become an ally of France, but (more importantly) because of an invitation from Protestant elements in the English Parliament. He crossed the Channel in the stormy November of 1688, landing at Torbay. A small number of English officers and soldiers defected to him but most remained loyal. James, however, had lost his nerve. He was convinced his own army would no longer fight for him, and he fled to France.

THE ARMY OF WILLIAM III

The accession of William and Mary was almost as much of a surprise to their supporters as to their opponents. It had been assumed that William's invasion would bring James to his senses, forcing him to protect the rights of Parliament and the supremacy of the Protestant religion, but leaving him as king. James's flight to the French court made this impossible, and England now found itself firmly locked into William's anti-French alliance.

The Scots and Irish were, however, far less willing to accept William and Mary. With French backing, James landed at Kinsale on 12 March 1689 and attempted to raise the Catholic Irish in his support. The army in Ireland consisted of a troop of Horse Guards, a troop of Horse Grenadier Guards, a regiment of Foot Guards, a regiment of dragoons, 8 of foot and 3 of horse. A large part of this force came over to James giving him some 7000 regulars. The Protestants in the ranks, however, refused to join James, and left their regiments for Londonderry, which endured a siege of 105 days until General Kirke relieved the town.

In August 1689, King William's main army landed in Ireland. It was made up of Dutch and Danish as well as English regiments. The army suffered terrible privations due to poor supply and ill discipline, and thousands died of

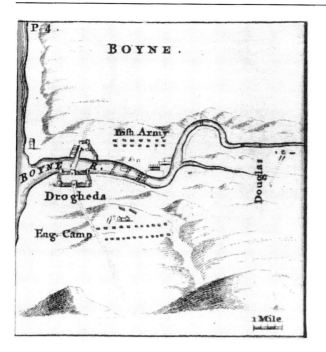

surprise attack on the French position at Steenkirk but the French commander, Luxembourg, quickly organised a defensive line of battle. The British infantry pushed the French back to their camp, but were, in turn, forced to retire when the French and Swiss Guards counter-attacked. The stolid bravery of the British infantry was already being recognised by Continental commanders. At the crucial point in the battle of Steenkirk, the Count of Solms refused English pleas for reinforcement with the words 'Damn the English. They are very fond of fighting; now let them have a bellyfull of it'. Both sides lost about 7000 men.

The following year the armies again clashed at Landen (Neerwinden). Luxembourg with 80,000 men attacked William's army of 50,000 in its defensive camp. Despite several repulses, the French were able to use their superior numbers to rout William's army; the British contingent fought particularly well and managed to retain enough order to conduct a steady fighting retreat. In 1697, with both sides exhausted by nine years of war, an unsatisfactory peace – effectively merely a cease-fire – was concluded. French expansionism resurfaced in 1701, with the outbreak of the War of Spanish Succession.

The battle of the Boyne (1 July 1690) saw 26,000 Jacobites overwhelmed by 35,000 Williamites including many Dutch and Danish veterans. William ordered Schomberg and then Douglas to mount a flanking attack on Slane bridge. James overreacted and sent his reserve to meet it. William then ordered a frontal assault across the river against the strong Jacobite positions. Bitter fighting resulted until William led his left-flank cavalry through bogs bordering the river. Finding themselves outflanked, the Jacobites began to withdraw under the cover of cavalry. Jacobite losses were not serious, but James fled back to France abandoning his followers. From The Wars of William III and Queen Anne by Brig-Gen Kane, 1735. (Private Collection)

sickness. Reinforcements were gathered for both armies and in July 1690, 35,000 Williamites defeated 26,000 Jacobites at the Boyne. James deserted his soldiers again and left for France. One by one the Jacobite garrisons were forced to surrender, so that by October 1691 the war in Ireland was over.

The European war

While William had been occupied in Ireland, the French war had been developing unabated. Churchill (the later Duke of Marlborough) led an 8000-strong English contingent to Flanders where they distinguished themselves at the indecisive battle of Walcourt. The French won the battle of Fleurs in July 1690, and in 1691 they captured Mons and Hal before defeating the Allies again at Lens. In 1692 William took personal command but could not prevent the fall of Namur. In August he mounted a

UNIFORMS & WEAPONS OF THE HORSE

The English Civil War had resolved the question of whether cavalry should rely on firepower or shock tactics: the charge home with sword was now standard. A pair of pistols remained in use – one fired during the charge and the other held in reserve for the pursuit or retreat. Carbines were not issued to all New Model Horse, although this may have been as much an economy measure as a reflection of tactical doctrine. Carbines continued to be issued in circumstances where they were of value, particularly for patrol or picket duties. Indeed there was a general move later in the century to re-arm horse with carbines, beginning with the Horse Guards.

The buffcoat remained a key part of the horseman's defensive armour though it was now sometimes worn under a top coat. From about the early 1690s buffcoats began to be replaced by waistcoats made of cloth – perhaps a case of comfort before safety. Back and breast plates remained in use for much of the period, though Oxford's Horse were ordered to discard their armour at the start of the 1688 campaign. The pot helmet or 'tri-bar' also remained in use for some time, although metal 'secrets' worn under hats were becoming popular by the 1690s.

The Horse Guards

While Charles II had been in exile on the Continent, a group of volunteer gentlemen had formed his mounted lifeguard of two troops. Following the Restoration a new mounted lifeguard was established made up of three troops of Horse Guards each 200 strong. These troops were known as the King's, the Duke of York's (composed of the two troops of old Royalists) and the Duke of Albemarle's (which became the Queen's on Albemarle's death in 1671). Recruits were drawn from the gentry and from men who had served the Royalist cause during the Civil Wars and the king's exile.

The earliest information on the dress of the Horse Guards comes from the Coronation in 1661 where Sir Edmund Walker describes them thus: '*The King's Horse Guard, all well mounted, having Buffe Coates, with white Armour, their Horses furnished with Hooses (being a short Foot cloth) with red Scarfes, & plumes of Red & white Feathers... The Guards of His Royal Highnesse the Duke of Yorke ... all haveing black Armour, Red, white & black Feathers, and Red Scarfes, with belts of his Highnesse Livery.*'

Regulations for musters in the *State Papers Domestic* describe the arms required for the Horse in 1663: '*Each Horseman to have for his defensive arms, back, breast, and pot, and for his offensive arms, a sword, a case of pistols the barrels whereof are not to be under 14 inches in length, and each trooper of Our Guards to have a carbine besides ...*'
The issue of carbines was clearly to be a specific feature of the Horse Guards.

As so often in this period it is unwise to assume that

In addition to two pistols, many horsemen carried a carbine which was normally suspended on a broad carbine belt worn over the right shoulder. The carbine was clipped to the belt by a ring fitted to a metal rail on the side of the carbine. This example has a 31-inch barrel and a bore of .67 inches. (National Army Museum)

The charge home with sword had been the normal tactic during the Civil War but on the Continent, where many of the new generation of officers learnt their trade, reliance on pistols continued. (Royal Armouries, Tower of London)

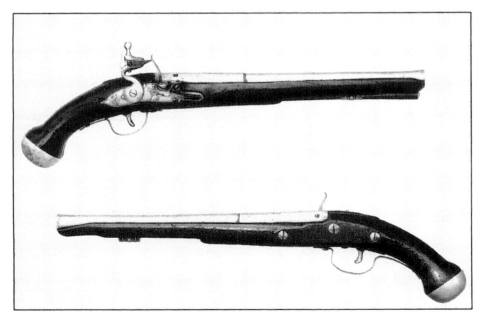

equipment was issued just because an order was given. In 1670 the Duke of Monmouth, then colonel of the King's Troop, wrote: '*I have taken an account of the arms of my troop and find that of 200 backs, breasts and potts, 50 are wanting, whereof 14 were lost, some at the fire at the Horse Guards and others in service at Winchcombe. I beg for their supply and for 200 carbines promised by HM to the troop.*' The letter appears to have had an effect, for on 16 September 1670, Monmouth wrote arranging for the delivery of the missing 200 carbines, complete with straps and sockets.

The next sighting of the Horse Guards is in *Travels of Cosmo III through England* dated 1669: '*The 1st of the Company (or Troops) of the body-guard called the King's Company, composed of gentlemen and half pay officers, dressed in red jackets (or coats) faced with blue and richly ornamented with gold lace and wearing white feathers in their hats was commanded by the Duke of Monmouth. The 2nd called the Duke's wore red jackets with blue facings without gold, and white feathers in their hats. The 3rd, that of the General, wore a dress similar to that of a Duke's, and instead of feathers a ribbon of crimson colour.*'

The most detailed description of the Horse Guards comes from the Coronation of James II in 1685 and is quoted in the commentary to Plate F1.

The Earl of Oxford's Horse

In 1660 the new Royalist government had intended to disband all of Cromwell's regiments and to leave the defence of the country in the hands of the navy and militia. Before this was completed, a group of religious extremists rose up in London in 1661. The militia was called out but demonstrated that it could not contain even the most limited civil disturbance, and regular soldiers had to be

This gentleman out hunting in the late 1660s demonstrates how closely military and civilian fashions followed one another. He wears a wide-brimmed beaver hat and a small cravat tied with a black ribbon. His coat has wide cuffs and fashionably short sleeves. The slits at the side and rear of his coat allow it to spread comfortably when on horseback. The high knee boots and spur are in the military jackboot style. His sword, a court small sword rather than a military double-edged cavalry sword, is worn on a heavily decorated baldrick. (Private Collection)

called in to restore order. As a result, the Cromwellian horse regiment of Unton Crook was reorganised rather than disbanded. It was placed under the command of Aubrey de Vere, the Earl of Oxford, and restyled 'The Earl of Oxford's Horse'.

The regiment was to consist of seven troops of 60 men and a king's troop of 80. These strengths appear not to have been reached as in 1677 an order was made that all troops of the regiment be recruited to 60 troopers. In a review of 1684 each troop contained only 3 corporals, 2 trumpeters and 45 troopers.

Troopers' coats and cloaks were of blue lined with red, to distinguish them from the Horse Guards; horse furniture and holsters were of blue embroidered with the Royal Cipher. Back and breast plates, pot helmets and carbines were issued to recruits joining the regiment in February 1678 indicating that existing troopers were already so equipped. In 1684 the troopers had 'their Carbine Belts laced with Gold upon Buff with a red edging'. A contemporary painting shows troopers in grey hats with black feathers. In November 1688, along with other regiments of horse, Oxford's men were ordered to abandon their armour as they marched to meet the invasion force of William of Orange. Buff leather waistcoats may have been worn up until 1696 when buff-coloured cloth waistcoats were issued.

The new regiments of 1685–88

The Monmouth rebellion gave James II an excuse to raise new regiments. Though the rising was crushed before

A heavy cavalry sword said to have been issued to the Earl of Oxford's Horse. Although primarily designed for lunging with the point, the double-edged blade could also be used for slashing. (Royal Armouries, Tower of London)

The Scottish troop of Horse Guards in 1685. A contract of 1699 records their uniform as 'one fashionable coat of fine scarlet cloth, lined with a white shalloon serge ... one waistcoat of blue cloth with lining ... one pair of breeches of the same cloth [as] the waistcoat, lined with teel [tweed] and having leather pockets'. From The Life Guards in the Procession at the opening of the first Parliament of James the Seventh (and Second) in Edinburgh, 1685, *an engraving by Thomas Summers. (Private Collection)*

recruitment had been completed, many of these new units were retained in service. Once the rebellion was over, each cavalry troop was reduced to 40 private troopers, perhaps achieved by putting an end to new recruiting. Many of the new units were disbanded almost immediately after they were raised. Lord Dover's new regiment was converted to a troop of the Horse Guards. The Queen's Regiment of Horse was raised by a royal warrant dated 13 June 1685 and was to consist of 9 troops each of 1 quartermaster, 60 soldiers, 3 corporals and 2 trumpeters besides commissioned officers. The following horse regiments seem also to have achieved, by 1686, a more permanent footing: the Queen Dowager's, the Earl of Peterborough's, the Earl of Plymouth's, the Earl of Thanet's, and the Earl of Scarsdale's.

As to the equipment of these regiments, on 15 June 1685 the following order had been issued: '*Equipment to be sent to Berwick to add to arms there to equip a regiment of Horse: Back and Breast and Potts 360 Carbines with Belts and Swivels 360 Pistolls with holsters 1440.*' This confirms that the new regiments were fully equipped with carbines and body armour, though the issue of double the normal proportion of pistols cannot be explained. An order for the issue of '*100 suits of Armour ... Brests to be Carbine proof and ye Backs and Potts Pistol proof*' indicates that the armour was of the same standard of protection as used during the Civil War and was not merely for show.

The horse retained uniforms in much the same style for the remainder of the century with broad cross-belts for carbine and sword worn over a crimson coat. The normal head dress was the wide-brimmed hat, usually with a 'secret' iron head protector worn underneath; the pot helmet was still worn in battle by some units as late as 1696.

The *London Gazette* of 30 June–4 July 1687 carried the following advertisement concerning the Queen's Horse:

'*Stolen from Nathaniel Green, Quartermaster a red coat with large plate buttons, lined with yellow silk, the sleeves faced with silver tissue, a silver net-fringed scarf, a pair of silver fringed gloves, a black hat laced and a silver hat-band, a white Holland waistcoat with a fringe, a periwig, etc ...*'

A warrant from around 1696 gives the following particulars of the clothing of a regiment of horse.

Clothing	Former price		
	£	s	d
300 Coats of Crimson Cloth	3	10	0
18 Coats of Crimson Cloth, Corporals	4	10	0
318 Cloaks of red cloth	2	5	0
318 Hats edged with silver	0	15	0
318 swords	0	10	0
318 Shoulder belts	0	10	0
318 Carbine belts	0	7	0
318 Cloth Waistcoats	0	1	5
318 Pr. Buff Gloves	0	7	6
318 Hoose and Caps, embroidered	1	5	0
318 Pr. Jack boots	1	6	0
318 Cartouch boxes	0	2	6

Memo: Each Captain clothes his own trumpeter and the Kettle drum is clothed by the Colonel.'

An order for 1696 specifies that the horse will be re-equipped every two years: '*The Troopers shall be completely clothed every two years; and care shall be taken that neither arms, Boots, Saddles nor any other accoutrements belonging either to the Trooper or Horse shall be wanting ... Officers to agree upon a pattern approved by the Colonel for their coats and to buy them where they like.*'

The 'secret' or iron skull cap was a common substitute for the helmet, especially from the 1690s. It was worn fitted inside the hat. The version on the right has holes so that it could be sown into the hat band. (National Army Museum)

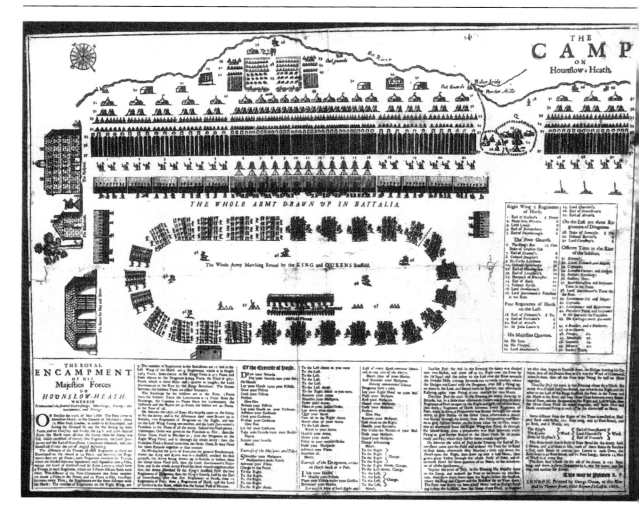

THE CAMP on Hounflow·Heath.

THE WHOLE ARMY DRAWN UP IN BATTALIA

The Whole Army Marching Round by the KING and QUEENS Scaffold.

THE ROYAL ENCAMPMENT OF HIS Majeftics Forces AT HOUNSLOW·HEATH.

DRAGOONS

The dragoon had proved a popular troop type during the Civil War. Although fighting on foot as an infantryman, the dragoon's mobility made him ideal for scouting, picket duty and for collecting taxes, and supplies from enemy territory. The Restoration Army had no need for these services, and the anti-military feeling of Parliament, in any case, made the raising of dragoons difficult politically.

It was not until April 1672 that Prince Rupert's Regiment of Dragoons was raised. It was to consist of 12 troops each of 80 men: *'that is to say, three corporals, two serjeants, the gentleman of arms, and 12 soldiers of each of the said 12 Troops, are to have and carry each of them one halbard, and one case of pistols with holster; and the rest of the soldiers ... are to have and to carry each of them one matchlock musquet, with a collar of bandaleers, and also to have and carry one bayonet, or great knife: That each*

James II instituted summer camps, often on Hounslow Heath, at which the army was brought together for training and inspection. These became a regular feature of army life, and a political gesture aimed at keeping Parliament in its place. Print by G. Croom, dated 1686 (National Army Museum)

lieutenant have and carry one partizan; and that two drums be delivered out for each Troop.'

The use of matchlock muskets and bandoleers was unusual; experience during the Civil Wars had led to New Model dragoons being armed with flintlocks and cartridge boxes which were easier to manage on horseback. The 1672 regiment was, however, soon disbanded. When war threatened again in 1678, another regiment of dragoons was raised for Prince Rupert. Each troop was to consist of 1 captain, 1 lieutenant, 1 quarter-master, 2 sergeants, 3 corporals, 2 drummers, and 80 'private soldiers' to be armed with '2 Partisans, 6 Halberts, 12 Fusils, 68 Musquets (with slings to all the firearms), 80 Cartridge-boxes, 80 Bayonets, 6 cases of pistols, 2 Drums'. In the same month, orders were issued that all the firearms were to be snaphances.

Until this date, dragoon regiments had been raised for service in particular campaigns and disbanded immediately afterwards; the first permanent dragoon regiment was, like many of the army's early units, created almost by accident. In October 1661 a body of 109 horsemen had been sent from London to form part of the Tangier garrison. When Tangier was abandoned in 1683, the Tangier Horse returned to England and the four troops were combined with two independent troops of dragoons to form the Royal Regiment of Dragoons.

The new regiment was dressed in crimson coats for officers and red coats and cloaks lined blue for the men. Horse furniture and holsters were red with blue and yellow embroidery and bore the Royal Cipher. Each troop consisted of a captain, a lieutenant, a cornet, a quartermaster, 2 sergeants, 3 corporals, 2 hautbois, 2 drummers, and 50 private soldiers.

When new dragoons were raised during the Monmouth Rebellion they followed the standardised arming of the Royal Dragoons. '5 New troops of Dragoons' were raised, each troop with:

'Snaphance musquetts strapt for Dragoons	63
Cartouch Boxes with girdles	63
Boots or Socketts for ye muskets	63
Drummes for Draggoons	2
Byonetts with Froggs and Belts	63
Halberts [for sergeants]	2
Partizans [for captain and lieutenant]	2
Saddles	69'

An instruction of February 1687 states that dragoons should be equipped with: 'Snaphance Musquets, strapped, with bright barrels of 3 foot 8 inches long, cartouche boxes, bayonets, granade pouches, buckets, and hammer hatchets'.

In May 1678 two independent companies of dragoons were formed in Scotland and a third company was added in 1679. These men wore grey coats and bonnets and were armed with broadswords, short muskets with belts and pistols. In November 1681 a dragoon regiment, which later became known as the Scots Greys, was formed by adding three new companies to the existing three and reforming each to 50 men. The regiment continued to wear stone grey clothing until at least the end of 1684 and in June 1685 was ordered into England in response to the Monmouth

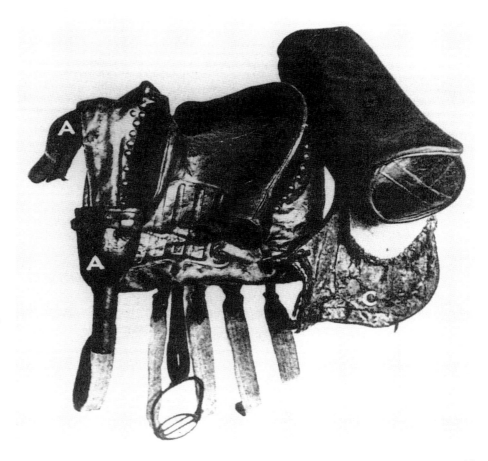

Said to have been used at Killiecrankie in 1689, this saddle illustrates the pistol holsters (marked A) and the firm support required to hold a horseman in the saddle when he crossed swords with an enemy. Some provision was also made for carrying personal equipment in the bag at the rear. (Private Collection)

Rebellion. A recent theory that the Scots Greys were so called from this grey clothing rather than from the colour of their horses seems to be contradicted by the following account from 1687. This details the materials used to manufacture red coats for the regiment, in a period long before the title 'Scots Greys' entered common usage:

	'Scots			English		
	£	s	d	£	s	d
5½ ells red cloth at £2 Scots per ell	11	0	0	0	18	4
6 ells blue serge lining at £1 scots per ell	6	0	0	0	10	0
1½ ell green canvas for bindings	0	4	0	0	0	4
10 dozen tin buttons at 5s per doz	2	10	0	0	4	2
10 drab weight red silk at 18d per drab	0	15	0	0	1	3
3 oz red thread at 3s per oz	0	9	0	0	0	9
—– to drab on the buttons	0	2	0	0	0	2
Making the coat	2	0	0	0	3	4
[Total]	23	0	0	1	18	4'

A Scottish ell measured 37 inches providing enough cloth for a coat loose enough to be worn over a waistcoat with the wide skirts necessary when mounted on a horse.

An order of 1697 sets out the provision of uniform for the dragoons: '*The Dragoons shall have every year one pair breeches, one hat; every two years one Coat of better cloth than usually, and one cap; every three years one Cloak, one Housing, one Saddlery and harness, with Swords, Bayonets, belts, Cartouch-box and slings.*' . . . '*Officers to agree upon a pattern approved by the Colonel for their coats and to buy them where they like.*'

A list of 1696 gives a detailed breakdown of a dragoon regiment's clothing:

	'Former price' (each)		
	£	s	d
411 Coats and breeches	2	2	0
483 Cloaks	2	0	0
467 Hats	0	8	6
467 Caps	0	5	0
467 Neckcloths	0	1	6
483 Pr. Boots	0	12	0
467 Waist belts	0	4	6
467 Swords	0	7	6
483 Leather Bags	0	4	0
467 Hoose and caps, embroidered	0	12	0
411 Daggers	0	2	6
411 Cartouch boxes	0	2	6
467 Pr. Stockings	0	2	0
16 Sergeants' coats and breeches	3	10	0
16 Hats	0	15	0
16 Caps	0	10	0
16 Cravats	0	2	6
16 Swords	0	10	0
16 Belts	0	6	0
16 Pr. Stockings	0	6	0
16 Hoose and caps	0	18	0
24 Corporals' suits	2	10	0
16 Drummers' suits	2	10	0
16 Hoboys' suits	3	10	0'

By the end of the century the dragoon was near the end of its existence as a troop type distinct from cavalry. A number of changes to the dragoon's equipment signalled the new role. In May 1690 a company of 'Grenadiers on horseback' of the 4th Dragoons were issued with grenade pouches and fusils. In September 1697 the 8th Dragoons (Cunningham's) had their pay docked to provide pistols. In actions such as the storming of the Schellenberg in

Towards the end of our period, the distinction between dragoon and cavalry declined as governments realised that the dragoon could fulfil many of the duties of the cavalryman but cost less in pay, mounting and equipment. This French dragoon carries his musket with its butt lodged in a 'bucket'; aside from this he might otherwise be taken for a cavalryman. Engraving by N. Guerard. (Private Collection)

1704, dragoons dismounted to take part in the attack; but in open battle they now fought normally on horseback – abandoning their old role as mounted infantry and becoming part of the cavalry arm.

INFANTRY UNIFORMS

The provision of uniform throughout our period remained the business of the regimental commander. The ordinary soldier paid for his uniform and equipment through regular deductions taken from his pay, called 'off reckonings'. He had no say in the quality of his uniform; and as his equipment and uniform wore out he was required to pay for replacements, putting him almost permanently into debt. In February of 1678 the following order was made for the provision of uniforms and equipment to NCOs, men and recruits raised for the war with France:

'For the new clothing with a cloth coat lined with baize, one pair of kearsey breeches, lined, with pockets, two shirts, two cravats, one pair of shoes, one pair of yarn hose, one hat, edged and hat band, one sash, and also one sword and belt ... the said clothing be satisfied for out of the off-reckonings of their pay, over and above their weekly subsistence-money, from time to time. And in case the said new-raised forces be disbanded before the off-reckonings reserved shall be sufficient to pay for the above clothing, what they fall short shall be paid out of Our treasure ... provided that the particulars before-mentioned do not exceed 53 shillings in the whole for each man.'

Though the uniform to be supplied was regulated centrally, it was left to the regiment to arrange manufacture. In 1690 the *London Gazette* published instructions to regiments: colonels were to appoint two or three officers to see patterns of cloth, lining, etc. and to haggle down the price as low as they could. The colonel, if he approved, was to make a contract with the tradesmen and to sign it together with all his captains.

For most of the period the colour of the coat was fixed as red; considerable leeway was given to commanders about other aspects such as linings. The Duke of Beaufort was told in a letter of 4 July 1685 concerning his new regiment: 'As to their Clothing, the outside being red, [His Majesty] leaves it to you to use what other colour you like best for the lining.'

The choice was not always made on sound military principles as Lord Chesterfield wrote in 1667: 'The soldiers red coats lined with black and black flags with a red cross in a black field, which I did, because I was at that time in mourning for my mother.' Some colonels found their

This Dutch musketeer retains the musket rest, which had been discarded in England during the Civil Wars, and wears a pot helmet of a kind rarely seen in England after 1642. His baggy breeches and long cassack, worn over a short doublet, were fashionable in the 1650s and early 1660s. (From Memorie der Particuliere Exercitie by Johan Boxel)

personal preferences overruled by the patron of their regiment. It is thought that the Lord Admiral's Regiment wore yellow coats lined red, which were the colours of the Duke of York who was admiral at the time.

In an attempt to maintain some standards of quality, patterns and cloth specimens were issued to the manufacturers and copies were kept for later comparison with the finished articles. That way at least it was hoped manufacturers would not shortchange soldiers by supplying shoddy clothing in small sizes. Two government 'patterns' were kept, one at the Tower, and one in the Strand, though unfortunately both sets were destroyed by fire, one in the 18th, the other in the 19th century. No other official record was kept.

Even if they had survived, these 'patterns' would tell only part of the story: changes to a regiment's uniform could occur at the whim of its commander following the latest fashion. In 1695 in order to check a growing fad for grenadier style caps King William issued an order that 'none of our regts. or companies of Foot do wear caps, excepting only the Royal Regiment of Fusileers, the Regt. of Scots Fusileers, and the Grenadeers of each respective regiment'.

At the end of the War of the Grand Alliance in 1697 the allocation of uniform and equipment was still much as it had been in 1678: *'One suit of clothes shall be taken every year out of the off-reckonings in the infantry, the first year one coat, 1 pr. breeches, one cap or hat, two shirts, two Cravats, two pairs of stockings and two pairs of shoes, the second year one Surtoute, one pair of breeches, one Shirt, one Cravat, one pair of stockings and one pair of shoes. And give the whole regiment every three years what they call the small armament Vizt. one Sword, one Bayonet, one Belt, one Cartridge Box with the furniture and slings.' 'Officers to agree upon a pattern approved by the Colonel for their coats and to buy them where they like.'*

The general demobilisation at the end of the war saw many soldiers returning to civilian life with the items that they had paid for from their off-reckonings: *'That the non-commissioned Officers and Soldiers be permitted to carry away with them their cloaths belt and snapsack, and the Serjeants likewise their sword; and that each private soldier, corporal, and drummer be allowed 3s. for his sword.'*

Military musicians from 1670. They have the arms of their commander emblazoned on their drums and the Royal Arms on a fife banner. Two of them wear cravats, though the others still have 'falling band' collars.

Unlike the musicians, the officer (far right) has fashionable sleeves cut short to the elbow and wears a sash over his shoulder. From Funeral of the Duke of Albemarle, *1670. (British Museum)*

Officers

During the Civil Wars officers had worn their own clothing rather than a regimental uniform and this custom continued after the Restoration. Regulations for officers' clothing were introduced only gradually, and throughout the period remained as much a matter of fashion as of military discipline.

In 1684 an order was made designating the style of gorget to denote officer ranks: *'For the better distinction of Our several Officers serving in Our Companies of Foot, Our will and pleasure is, that all Captains of Foot wear no other Corselet [i.e. gorget] than of the colour of gold; all Lieutenants, black corselets studded with gold, and the Ensigns corselets of silver. And we do likewise think fit that all Lieutenants of Foot carry pikes and not partisans, which we do hereby order to be returned into the office of Our Ordnance.'*

The success of this instruction may be judged from the following quotes. By the Coronation in April 1685 the officers of the First Foot Guards wore regulation gorgets and despite the finery on display there was a clear move towards scarlet as the colour of an officer:
'The Officers of this First Regiment of Foot-Guards . . . were exceedingly richly Habited; some in Coats of Cloth of Gold, others in Crimson Velvet Imbroidered or Laced with Gold or Silver; but most of them in Fine Scarlet Cloth, Buttoned down the Brest and on the Facings of the Sleeves with Silver Plate.

Their Scarffs (which they wore about their wastes) were either Network of Gold or Silver, or Crimson Taffeta richly Fringed with Gold or Silver, and their Hats were adorned with Tours of White Feathers.

The Captains were distinguished by Corselets or Gorgets of Silver Plate double gilt; The Lieutenants by Corselets of Steel Polished and Sanguin'd, and Studded with Nails of Gold; and the Ensigns had their corselets of Silver Plate.'

The accession of William III caused a temporary shift away from red as the standard uniform colour, a move reflected in officers' dress. In 1691/2, the officers of Stewart's Regiment wore blue coats, lined with blue shalloon and decorated with gold. Abraham Creighton's and Gustavus Hamilton's officers had coats of scarlet broadcloth lined with scarlet shalloon and decorated with gold and silver. Lord Cutts', the Earl of Drogheda's, Coote's and Rowe's officers all had coats of crimson cloth lined with crimson shalloon.

By the early 1690s officers' uniforms were purchased on a regimental basis at least while on active service. In 1702, in instructions for the forthcoming campaign in Flanders, the Duke of Marlborough made it clear that officers' dress was to be uniform: *'That the officers be all clothed in red, plain and uniform, which is expected they shall wear on all marches and other duties as well as days of Review, that no officer be on duty without his regimental scarf and spontoon, and whereas the officers of some regiments have pikes and others spontoons, 'tis ordered that all provide spontoons according to the pattern which I have given to Major-General Sabine.'*

Soldiers' uniforms

Details of the early Restoration uniforms are scarce but it appears that the red coat was quickly confirmed as the standard dress of the British soldier. A receipt of 25 October 1661 records expenditure by Lord Wentworth on his regiment of Guards then in Dunkirk for 783 red tunics (probably for musketeers), 505 buff coats for pikemen and 1286 hats. This regiment was amalgamated with the First Foot Guards in 1665. When seen by Duke Cosmo in 1669 this regiment's musketeers wore red coats turned up with light blue, and the pikemen coats of 'silver' colour turned up light blue. The Coldstream Guards had red coats lined green for musketeers and green lined red for pikemen. Distinguishing colours may also have been used on equipment: in 1667 the Coldstreams were issued with 650 collars of bandoleers covered with black leather and 'green strings'.

We have no reliable pictorial evidence of the style of coat worn by foot soldiers in the early years of the Restoration. Hollar's drawings of Tangier demonstrate that by 1669 a French-style, knee-length coat was being worn; with minor changes this remained the standard uniform coat for the rest of the period. At first the coat was worn loose with crossed bandoleer and shoulder belt, but in the mid-1670s a waist sash was introduced for both

These tiny figures in an etching by Hollar from sketches made at Tangier in 1669 show that the knee-length French-style coat had already been introduced into the English army. The coat has buttons all the way down to the hem, wide turnbacks on the sleeves, and is worn open under a bandoleer and sword baldrick, both some four inches wide. (From **Divers Prospects** in and about Tangier, exactly delineated by W. Hollar, His Majesties Designer)

pikemen and musketeers. The sash gave the coat a distinct pinched waist, a style that remained the norm until the early 1680s when musketeers abandoned the sash to wear their swords on waist belts rather than baldricks.

The First Foot Guards at the 1685 Coronation were uniformed as follows: *'The Private Soldiers were all new Cloathed in Coats of Red broad Cloth, Lined and Faced with Blew; Their Hats were Black, Laced about with Silver, turned up and garnished with Blew Ribbands. Their Breeches were Blew Broad Cloth, and their Stockings of Blew Worsted. The Musquetiers were Armed with Snaphance Musquets, with Sanguin'd Barrels, 3 Foot 8 Inches in length; good Swords in Waste Belts, and Collars of Bandiliers; And the Pike-men with Pikes 16 Foot long, each headed with a Three-Square Point of Steel, and good swords in broad Shoulder-belts, wearing also about their wastes, Sashes, or Scarffs of White Worsted, Fringed Blew.'*

Although red was the customary colour of soldiers' coats it was not universal. The Lord High Admiral's Regiment wore yellow coats lined red from their formation in 1664, but converted to red coats lined yellow when they became Prince George of Denmark's Regiment in 1685.

The Earl of Bath's Regiment formed during the Monmouth Rebellion wore blue coats lined red, but in 1691 changed to red coats just as a number of new regiments were being raised in blue coats for the Irish campaign. Lord Lindsay's Regiment which was on the Scottish establishment from 1694 to 1697 clad its Private Sentinels in coats and breeches of white Galloway cloth, and the sergeants in coats of stone grey and red breeches. In general, however, the end of the campaigns in Ireland, and the transfer of regiments to Flanders, saw a return to the red coat as the mark of the British soldier.

Waistcoats

The waistcoat presents a problem as in illustrations and eyewitness descriptions its presence or absence is hidden by the coat. Part of the difficulty is that the waistcoat was made from the previous year's uniform coat and so does not appear on warrants or bills. That this was standard practice is confirmed by Marlborough's order of 1702: '*And whereas a complaint has been made about the expense in turning the soldier's coats into waistcoats, 'tis ordered that all Colonels do the same out of the clothing money.*'

It is not known what arrangements were made for newly raised regiments or for recruits who in their first year of service would not have had an old coat to convert into a waistcoat. We do not know when waistcoats were first worn, but one of the earliest references comes from 1688 with the celebrations on the birth of a son to King James. The soldiers garrisoning Carlisle began 'throwing their hats into the fire at one health, their coats at the next, their waistcoats at a third'. Waistcoats were often the same colour as the lining of the uniform coat and it seems that the old coat was disassembled, with the clean inner face between cloth and lining becoming the new outer face. Waistcoats could be either sleeved or sleeveless, though any new sleeves had to be closely cut so that they could be worn under the coat sleeves.

The protection afforded by the two layers of the coat and waistcoat proved insufficient for service in Ireland. Dutch soldiers serving there were provided with 'surtouts' which would later be called 'greatcoats'. Some 'watch coats' were usually provided for each regiment to be issued to men on sentry duty, though in 1689, 15,000 'Surtoot White Coats' were sent to Ireland in addition to uniform coats for new regiments being raised. Another type of soldier's coat features in descriptions from the 1670s to 1700s. This is a grey coat often with black lining that appears to have been a fatigue or undress coat. For example, a deserter of Cornwall's Regiment in 1687 is described as wearing a grey coat lined black; another deserter from the Coldstreams in 1705 wore a grey coat trimmed blue.

INFANTRY WEAPONS & EQUIPMENT

In 1660 the standard offensive weapon for a pikeman was 16-foot pike; and for a musketeer, a matchlock musket with a set of bandoleers containing gunpowder. By 1704, the infantryman had a flintlock musket with his ammunition in paper cartridges kept in a cartridge box, and a socket bayonet to protect him from cavalry. These changes were partly responsible for a major improvement in infantry firepower, and for the continued development of new tactics based upon firepower to the exclusion of hand-to-hand combat.

From matchlock to flintlock

It had long been recognised that the matchlock was not suited to mounted use; costly and cumbersome wheel-lock pistols and carbines had to be produced instead. The Civil Wars saw these weapons gradually replaced by flintlock pistols and carbines for horse, while dragoons were issued with special flintlock muskets.

Though the flintlock was undoubtedly a superior weapon, its advantages over the matchlock have long been hugely overestimated by historians. Our knowledge of the performance of the flintlock comes mainly from trials held in the late 18th and early 19th centuries; no such trials are recorded for the matchlock. Modern comparison is based upon calculations of how long it would take to carry out the motions described in contemporary drill books. It has been claimed that a matchlock would take three to five minutes to load and fire while the same could be achieved with a flintlock in just 15 to 30 seconds. In fact drill manuals were training aids, not regulation procedures. Many 'postures' were illustrated as several distinct 'motions' to make them clearer. Unfortunately, different drill books contain different numbers of motions both for matchlock and flintlock drill, so direct comparison is difficult. By a happy chance the *Abridgement* of 1685 lists both matchlock and flintlock drill alongside each other. In all 32 motions are required to load and fire a matchlock, and 30 for the flintlock. The difference is a matter of a few seconds.

The accuracy of muskets depended upon the quality of the gunpowder and the gun barrel, as well as the tight fit of the bullet. Many flintlock muskets were merely old matchlocks fitted with new locks; so there is no reason for the flintlock to have been inherently more accurate. The matchlock did have one serious disadvantage in that it could only be used if the soldier had his match-cord alight

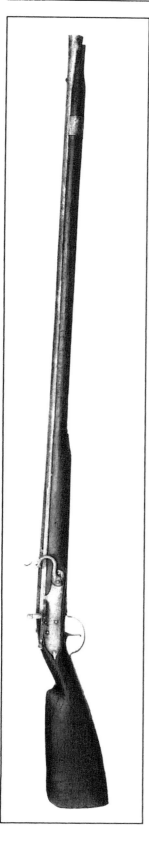

Sentries used large amounts of match to guard against surprise attack and this could cause problems if stocks were limited, as, for example, during prolonged sieges. The flintlock needed a steady supply of new flints as these were easily broken (though only when the weapon was in use). The discovery of sources of more resilient flints in the 17th century did much to improve reliability. Flintlock design also became more robust and James II was careful to specify that his Guards should be equipped with French locks – the best then available – for their muskets.

The one area in which the flintlock had a definite advantage was in volley fire. The matchlock was prone to a slow ignition, as the match did not always burn brightly enough to set off the priming charge at once: the flintlock gave a much more certain and immediate explosion and a unified volley. This had not mattered with early musketry tactics which concentrated on keeping up a continuous rolling fire. By the closing years of the century, new Dutch tactics called for carefully controlled volleys by bodies of musketeers, fired in rapid succession. For this type of drill the flintlock was far more effective.

The change-over from matchlock to flintlock muskets was a slow process. The slow and erratic progress of this change-over among British Guards regiments, and in particular, the Coldstream Regiment, has caused a considerable amount of debate in historical circles. In April 1660, Monk ordered four companies of his regiment (the future Coldstreams) to trade in their matchlocks for flintlocks. Yet only a few years later in February 1665, 500 guardsmen added to the regiment were equipped with matchlocks even though destined for service with the fleet. Several theories have been put forward to account for this apparently retrograde step – corruption, thrift, and plain stupidity. The puzzle does not stop there. In 1667 two new companies of the Coldstreams were issued with a mixture of matchlocks and flintlocks: 60 muskets with bandoleers and 13 firelocks. The flintlocks gained ground in May 1672

A late-17th-century matchlock musket. Unlike the version used in the English Civil Wars this example has the priming pan as part of the lock rather than the barrel. This made it easy to convert matchlocks to flintlocks by the simple expedient of changing the lock. (Royal Armouries, Tower of London)

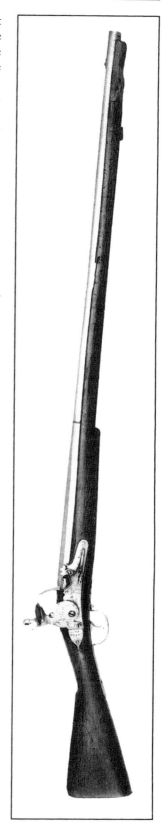

A late-17th-century flintlock musket. Although the term 'snaphance' was generally used by contemporaries to describe the flintlock, the true 'snaphance' was rarely seen in Britain. This highly decorated flintlock includes a 'dog' catch which secured the mechanism at 'half cock' preventing the flint from falling while the musket was being loaded. (Royal Armouries, Tower of London)

when recruits for nine companies of the Coldstreams were issued '91 snaphance musquets, 91 matchlock musquets, 182 collars of bandileers'. The conversion back to flintlocks became complete when in June 1683 the First Foot Guards, and in January 1684 the Coldstreams, were ordered to exchange their arms so that each company would carry 43 snaphance muskets and 20 pikes.

In terms of modernity of equipment, Guards regiments remained one step in advance of regular line regiments, and it was not until the end of the century that some units in remote outposts received replacements for their matchlocks. In September 1684 five companies of Trelawney's Regiment (withdrawn from Tangier) were re-equipped before going to Ireland, each company receiving: '20 long pikes, 12 snaphance muskets, 28 matchlocks, 40 collars of bandoleers'. In October two companies of the Holland Regiment in Jersey were to be armed with: '26 matchlock muskets, 9 snaphance muskets, 18 long pikes'.

The Lord High Admiral's Regiment served at sea and had been armed with flintlock muskets as the matchlock was considered a fire hazard on board ship. By 1685, the regiment was restyled the Prince of Denmark's Regiment, and converted into a line regiment. During the expansion of the army as a result of the Monmouth rebellion each company received: '28 matchlock muskets, 6 snaphance muskets, 16 long pikes, 34 bandoliers'. At the same time an order was made for the 10 companies of the newly raised Duke of Beaufort's Regiment to be issued with 590 matchlock muskets, 120 snaphance muskets, 320 long pikes and 710 bandoleers.

It is clear that the change from matchlock to flintlock was a gradual process, and the advantages of the flintlock had be weighed up at each stage against the additional cost. The length of time for the change-over indicates that the disadvantages of the matchlock were not as great as some historians have made out.

Bandoleers and cartridges

Although in the late 17th century the bandoleer was replaced by the cartridge box, the cartridge was by far the earlier invention. From medieval times a twist of paper had been the usual way of selling and carrying any powder, but this was vulnerable to damp, and the powder liable to leak out. The powder flask was introduced as a safer container, but had the disadvantage that even with a complicated spout arrangement it was difficult to ensure that a correctly measured charge was poured into the musket barrel. The 'collar of bandoleers' with its hanging wooden or metal 'boxes' each drilled to contain exactly the right charge solved the problem. Bandoleers had their own drawbacks: horsemen found that they bounced up and down with the motion of the horse, and grenadiers were concerned that

their burning grenade fuses might set off their bandoleers. Horse soldiers preferred flasks or cartridge boxes attached to their belt or saddle, and grenadiers also turned to the cartridge box worn on a waist belt. The dragoons of the New Model Army adopted the cartridge box in 1645.

Efforts were made to overcome the problem of the paper cartridges leaking their contents. Since little could be done about the paper the answer was to strengthen the cartridge box. An order of 1662 for the Irish 'Battle Axe Guard' contains the following specification: *'Tyn [i.e. tin] Cartouch boxes covered with Leather of Calves Skin for Musketts with Formers, prymeing boxes and neate [i.e. cows] leather girdles with white metal buckles 64 at 3s 6d.'*

The cartridge box was made of tin for strength and covered in leather to keep out damp. The 'Formers' mentioned above were wooden sticks around which the paper was rolled to give a cartridge of the correct length and diameter to hold the correct charge; the loaded paper cartridges were then usually secured with twine. The priming box held the finer powder needed for the touch pan of the musket. The drill for grenadiers set down in 1685 indicates that these small priming flasks were kept in the cartridge box rather than on a cord as were those of bandoleer-equipped musketeers. The girdle or waist belt was to be made from neate's (cow's) leather with a white or bright silver buckle rather than one painted black to protect it from rust.

The bayonet and the pike

The slow adoption of the bayonet – from its early recorded use by the English in the garrisons at Dunkirk and Tangier in 1662 and 1663, until widespread issue in the first decade of the 1700s – suggests that it too, like the flintlock musket, was not seen as an innovation that would immediately change the nature of infantry tactics. At first only specialist troops, without the protection of pikemen, were issued with bayonets. Dragoons raised in 1672 and grenadiers from their inception in 1677 were both issued with 'plug' bayonets, so called because the hilt plugged the muzzle of the musket. The first regiments with pikemen to be issued with bayonets were the Guards in 1686. Line regiments were equipped with bayonets only in a piecemeal fashion, and some regiments under Marlborough in the 1700s still had not received their issue.

Cost was a major factor in the speed of introduction, but the bayonet was obviously not considered so effective that regiments without them would be seriously disadvantaged in combat. That the plug bayonet prevented the musketeer firing his weapon was another major hindrance. The disaster which befell government forces at Killiecrankie in 1689 was attributed, quite falsely, to the plug bayonet. Heavy losses sustained in Ireland from cavalry

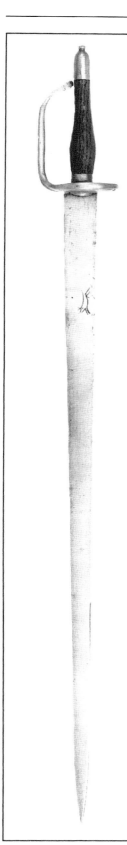

The 'sword bayonet' aimed to combine the advantages of the infantryman's hanger with those of the plug bayonet, but at 1 lb 4 oz in weight, made the musket unwieldy and unbalanced. The adoption of the socket bayonet effectively ended experiments of this kind. The blade is marked with a 'running wolf' – the mark of the blade makers of Solingen. By the late 17th century, many Germans were working from weapons factories that they established at Hounslow near London. (Royal Armouries, Tower of London)

Right and below: Charles II's departure from Scheveningen in Holland in May 1660. The painting is usually said to show red-coated British Foot Guards. However, the etching of the same scene by Nicolaus Visscher identifies these soldiers as Dutch. The painting copies the engraving. The artist may have chosen to paint the soldiers' coats red, the colour he saw being worn in London. (Private Collection)

attacks on Danish regiments armed with bayonets but no pikes, also did little to encourage adoption.

Efforts were made to overcome the disadvantages of the plug bayonet, particularly in France. Louis XIV watched a demonstration by his Guards using an improved bayonet secured to the side of the barrel by rings. Unfortunately when the Guards fired a volley many of the bayonets fell off; Louis XIV was not impressed, but experiments continued. The answer came finally with the 'socket bayonet' – secured by a slot that locked into a lug on the barrel, allowing the musket to be loaded and fired with bayonet in place. This tipped the scales in favour of the bayonet and the pike fell into disuse at the start of the 18th century.

Standardisation of equipment

During King James's reign, special efforts were made to standardise the equipment used by the army. These efforts

are particularly well summarised in the regulations for musters of 21 February 1687:

'The Musqueteers of our regiment of Foot-Guards to have Snaphance Musquets, with bright barrels, of 3 foot 8 inches long in the barrel, with good swords, bandoliers, and bayonets; and the Pikemen (as also the Pikemen of all other regiments) to have pikes 16 feet long, with good swords. Musquetiers of all other regiments of Foot (excepting our

Table A: Uniforms of the army reviewed at Putney Heath, 1684

The Horse Guards

Troop	Coats & Cloaks	Carbine belts	Grenadiers	Men
King's Troop	Scarlet lined blue	Velvet laced gold & silver; red hooses & holster caps embroidered with royal cipher & crown	Red coats, lined blue with blue loops tufted yellow; Caps lined the same and blue round mark on the outside	200
Queen's Troop	Scarlet lined blue	Green velvet laced gold; green hooses & holster caps embroidered with same cipher and crown	Green loops with yellow tufts	200
Duke's Troop	Scarlet lined blue	Velvet laced silver on yellow; hooses & holster caps embroidered on yellow, with same cipher and crown as the King's	Yellow coat loops	200

The Horse and Dragoons

Regiment	Coats & Cloaks	Carbine belts	Saddle Cloths	Troops	Men
Earl of Oxford's House	Blue lined red	Laced with gold on buff with a red edging; hooses & holster caps with royal cipher embroidered on blue.	(Unknown)	8	360
Royal Regt. of Dragoons	Red lined blue		Embroidered blue and yellow on red with the royal cipher; caps the same with royal cipher	6	300

The Foot

Regiment	Coats	Stockings	Breeches	Sash	Coys	Grenadier caps
Foot Guards	Red lined blue	Blue	Blue	White fringed blue	25	Lined blue, tufted blue & red, with royal cipher crowned
Coldstream Guards	Red lined green		Red	White fringed green	13	Lined green, with green tassels
Royal Regiment	Red lined white	Light grey	Light grey	White fringed white	21	Lined white, 'the lions face proper' crowned
Queen's Regiment					11	
Admiral's Regiment	Yellow lined red				12	
Holland Regiment	Red lined flesh colour				12	
Duchess of York's Regt.					11	

Source: *A General and Compleat List Military ... As Established at the time of the review upon Putney Heath the First of October 1684* by Nathan Brooks

The Restoration period
1: Trooper, King's Troop of Horse Guards, 1661
2: Musketeer, Lord Wentworth's Foot Guards, 1661
3: Pikeman, Coldstream Regiment of Foot Guards, 1669

A

The regimental tailor at work, 1686
1: Regimental tailor
2: Soldier, Prince George of Denmark's Regiment of Foot
3: Officer, Earl of Oxford's Horse
4: Soldier

B

Tangiers
1: Officer of the garrison, 1669
2: Musketeer, Governor's Regiment, 1669
3: Drummer, Coldstream Guards, 1671

C

The Virginia Colonies, 1677
1: Musketeer, Lord Admiral's Maritime Regiment of Foot
2: Pikeman, Coldsteam Regiment of Foot Guards
3: Grenadier, Colonel Herbert Jeffery's Regiment of Foot

D

Sedgemoor, 1685
1: Dragoon, Royal Regiment of Dragoons
2: General officer
3: Piper, Earl of Dumbarton's Regiment of Foot

E

The regiments of horse at Sedgemoor, 1685
1: Trooper, First Troop of Horse Guards
2: Trooper, Earl of Oxford's Horse
3: Horse grenadier, First Troop of Horse Grenadiers

F

The campaigns in Ireland
1: Musketeer, Lord Cutt's Regiment of Foot, King William's Army 1691
2: Pikeman, Earl of Bath's Regiment of Foot, King William's Army 1691
3: Trooper, Galmoy's Regiment of Horse, King James' Army 1692

G

Artillery
1: Fuzileer, Royal Regiment of Fuzileers, 1685
2: Gunner, The Train of Artillery in Ireland, King William's Army, 1689
3: Gunner, The Train of Artillery in Flander, 1695
4: Pioneer, The Train of Artillery, King James' Army, 1688

Regiment of Fusiliers, the Granadiers, and the company of Miners) to have Matchlock and Snaphance Musquets; the barrels whereof to be 3 foot 6 inches long, good swords, and bandoliers. Our Royal Regiment of Fusiliers to have Snaphance Musquets, strapped, with bright barrels of 3 foot 8 inches long, with good swords, cartouch boxes, and bayonets. All the Foot Granadiers of Our Army, both regimented and non-regimented, to have long carbines, strapped; the barrels whereof to be 3 foot 2 inches long, cartouche boxes, bayonets, granade pouches, and hammer hatchets. The Company of Miners to have long carabines, strapped; the barrels to be 3 foot 2 inches in length, cartouche boxes, bayonets, and extraordinary hammer hatchets. The Dragoons to have Snaphance Musquets, strapped, with bright barrels of 3 foot 8 inches long, cartouche boxes, bayonets, granade pouches, buckets, and hammer hatchets.'

The standardisation of military affairs begun by James did not continue into the reign of William and Mary when the introduction of Dutch ideas and the pressures of war caused a diverse variety of equipment to enter service. In March 1689 Beveridge's Foot were issued with equal numbers of matchlocks and flintlocks. In April 1690 the two new regiments of Pembroke and Torrington each received 1896 Dutch snaphance muskets, bayonets and cartridge boxes with girdles. In December 1695 the number of pikemen in a company was reduced to 14, as against 46 musketeers, being effectively the conversion of one six-man file.

Table B: James II's army on Hounslow Heath, 1686

Regiment	Clothing colour	Number of Troops/Coys.	Men each	Total
Horse on the right				
Earl of Oxford	Blue lined red	9	50	450
Maj-Gen Worthen's	Red lined red	6	40	240
Queen Dowager's	Red lined green	6	40	240
Earl of Shrewsbury's	Red lined buff	6	40	240
Earl of Peterborough's	Red lined red	6	40	240
Foot				
The 1st Bn, under Col. Stradling	Red lined with blue, blue breeches and stockings	7, one of them grenadiers	80	560
The King's 3rd Bn. under Cpt. Reresby	As above	6	80	480
Earl of Craven's 1st Bn. under Maj Hewit	Red lined blue, blue breeches, white stockings	6, plus a half coy of grenadiers	80	520
1st Bn. of Scotch Guards, under Maj. Murray	Red lined white, white breeches & stockings	7	80	560
Prince George's	Red lined yellow, grey breeches & stockings	12	50	600
Col. Oglethorpe's	Red lined ash, ash coloured breeches & stockings	12	50	600
Earl Huntingdon's	Red lined yellow, yellow breeches, grey stockings	10	50	500
Earl of Litchfield's	Red lined white, blue breeches & stockings	10	50	500
Marq. of Worcester's	Red lined tawny, tawny breeches & stockings	10	50	500
Earl of Bath's	Blue lined red, breeches & stockings	10	50	500
Col. Kirk's	Red lined green, green breeches, white stockings	10	50	500
Earl of Dumbarton's	Red lined white, grey breeches & stockings	11	50	550
Earl of Plymouth's	Red lined green	6	40	240
Horse on the left				
Earl of Scarsdale's	Red lined yellow	6	40	240
Earl of Arran's	Red lined white, with white silk sashes	6	40	240
The Queen's	Red lined yellow	6	40	240
Dragoons				
The King's		6	40	240
Princess of Denmark's		6	40	240
The Queen's		6	40	240
The Fuzileers	Red lined yellow, grey breeches & stockings	12 (one of miners)	50	600

Source: A List of King James's Army on Hounslow Heath, as they lay encamped ... June 30th 1686.

GRENADIERS

In May 1677 an order was issued that two soldiers from each company of the Guards regiments were to be trained as grenadiers. Accordingly the ten companies of the Coldstream Regiment each received 20 grenadier pouches, 20 hatchets and girdles and 20 'Fusees' or flintlock muskets. In April 1678 an order was made that a company of grenadiers consisting of 1 captain, 2 lieutenants, 3 sergeants, 3 corporals and 100 privates be added to each of the eight senior foot regiments of the army. Their arms were to be '103 Fusees with slings, 103 cartridge-boxes with girdles, 103 grenade pouches, 103 bayonets, 103 hatchets with girdles to them, 3 halberds (for sergeants) and 2 partisans (for officers)'. The muskets issued are specified elsewhere as 'long carbines strapped; the barrels whereof to be 3 foot 2 inches long'; the straps allowed the musket to be slung over the grenadier's back while he was using his hatchet or throwing a grenade.

As grenadier companies had no pikemen and were often stationed in advance, or on the wings of the regiment, they were issued bayonets for protection against cavalry. It appears that grenadiers were not at first issued swords though the evidence is contradictory. As the grenadier carried his four bombs in a pouch slung over his left shoulder his cartridges were kept in a pouch on his waist belt.

The first description of the British grenadier comes from John Evelyn's diary in June 1678. He describes them as 'new sort of soldiers with a pouch full of hand grenades'. They wore 'furred caps with coped crowns like Janizaries, which gave them a fierce expression: while some wore long hoods hanging down behind, as fools are pictured. Their clothing was piebald, yellow and red.' Two different styles of cap are described, one with a high crown and a fur edging, and another with a hanging bag. Both types appear in French illustrations of the period, and were probably devised by the regiments themselves.

The most detailed early description is of the grenadiers of the First Foot Guards at James II's coronation in 1685: '*The Granadiers (viz. Two Companies) were Cloathed*

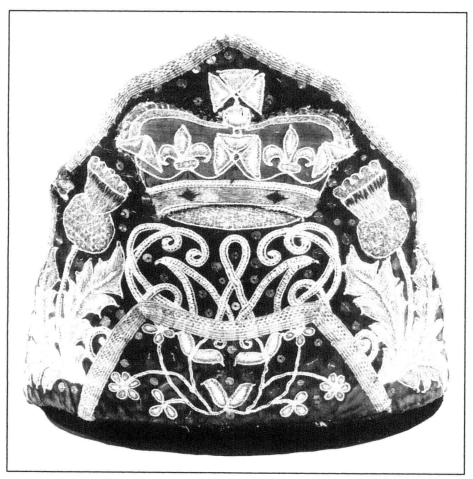

A grenadier officer's mitre cap of c.1690. Officers still had a large degree of freedom in their choice of uniform, and grenadier company officers seem to have copied the unusual style of dress of their men. The grenadier cap appeared in various styles: with hanging bags or hoods, high conical points with tassels, or as decorated caps. This example is some eight inches tall and is decorated with thistles denoting Scottish origins. (Scottish United Services Museum)

as the Musquetiers, but distinguished by Caps of Red Cloth Lined with Blew Shallon, and Laced with Silver Galoon about the Edges: And on the Frontlets of said Caps (which were very large and high) was Imbroidered the Kings Cipher and crown. Each of these Granadiers was Armed with a long Carabine Strapt, the Barrel thereof 3 Foot 2 Inches in length: a cartouch-box, Bionet, Granada-Pouch, and a Hammer-Hatchet.' On the same occasion, the Coldstream Regiment's grenadiers had caps lined and faced with 'Blew Chaloon, and Laced with Gold Galoon, and Imbroidered on the Frontlets with the Kings Cipher'.

Bibliography

Allingham, A., *A Treatise of Military Orders, and the Art of Gunnery, or throwing of Bombs, Balls, etc.* (London 1722)

Barthorp, Michael, *British Cavalry Uniforms since 1660* (Poole 1984)

Barthorp, Michael, *British Infantry Uniforms since 1660* (Poole 1982)

Beddard, Robert, *A Kingdom without a King* (London 1988)

Blackmore, H. L., *British Military Firearms 1650–1850* (London 1961)

Brooks, Nathan, *A General and Complete List Military of Every Commission Officer of Horse and Foot now commanding in his Majesty's Land Forces of England* (London 1684)

Carman, W. Y., *British Military Uniforms from Contemporary Pictures* (London 1957 & 1968)

Childs, John, *The Army of James II* (London 1976)

Childs, John, *The Army, James II and the Glorious Revolution* (Manchester 1980)

Childs, John, *Armies and Warfare in Europe 1648–1789* (Manchester 1982)

Childs, John, *The British Army of William III 1698–1702* (Manchester 1987)

Childs, John, *The Nine Years' War and the British Army 1688–97* (Manchester 1991)

Dalton, Charles, *English Army Lists and Commission Registers 1660–1714*, Vol. I (London 1892)

Dalton, Charles, *The Scots Army 1661–1688* (London 1909 & 1989)

Davis, John, *The History of the Second Queen's Royal Regiment*, Vol. I (London 1887)

Ede-Borrett, Stephen, *The Army of James II, Uniform and Organisation* (Leeds 1987)

Field, Cyril, *Old Times Under Arms, A Military Garner* (London 1939)

Fortescue, J. W., *A History of the British Army* Vol. I (London 1910)

Dutch pikemen of the early 1660s retain their helmets, back and breast plates, with short 'tassets' protecting the thighs. In England armour was discarded during the Civil Wars but there were efforts to reintroduce it during Cromwell's rule. (From the Dutch manual Drilkonst by Hendrik van Buren)

Grant, Charles Stewart, *From Pike to Shot 1685 to 1720* (Wargames Research Group, 1986)

Halkett, Sir James, *A Short and True Account of the most remarkable things that passed during the late Wars with the Moors at Tangier in the year 1680 etc.* (JSAHR special issue, 1922)

Houlding, J. A., *Fit for Service: The Training of the British Army 1715–1795* (Oxford 1981)

Kane, Richard, *Campaigns of King William and the Duke of Marlborough* (London 1747)

Kemp, Anthony, *Weapons & Equipment of the Marlborough Wars* (Poole 1980)

Journal of the Society for Army Historical Research (JSAHR), various articles since 1921.

Lawson, Cecil C. P., *A History of the Uniforms of the British Army*, Vol. I (London 1940 & 1969)

Luttrell, Narcissus, *A Brief Historical Relation of State Affairs*, Vol. I (Oxford 1857)

MacDonald Wigfield, W., *The Monmouth Rebellion, A Social History* (Bradford-on-Avon 1980)

Mackinnon, Daniel, *Origin and Service of the Coldstream Guards* (London 1833)

Magolotti, Count Lorenzo, *The Travels of Cosmo the Third, Grand Duke of Tuscany, through England ... 1669* (London 1821)

National Army Museum, *1688 Glorious Revolution? The Fall and Rise of the British Army 1660–1704* (exhibition catalogue) (London 1988)

Petard, Michel, *Equipements Militaires de 1600, 1870,* Vol. I (no date)

Routh, E. M. G., *Tangier, England's Lost Atlantic Outpost 1661–1684* (London 1912)

Sapherson, C. A., *The British Army of William III* (Leeds 1987)

Sapherson, C. A., *William III at War, Scotland & Ireland 1689–1691* (Leeds 1987)

Scott, Sir Sibbald David, *The British Army: its Origin, Progress, and Equipment,* Vol. 3 (London 1880)

Tincey, John, *Armies of the Sedgemoor Campaign* (Leigh on Sea: Partizan Press, 1985)

Tincey, John (ed.), *Monmouth's Drill Book: An abridgement of the English Military Discipline 1676* (Leigh on Sea: Partizan Press, 1986)

Trenchard, Thomas, *A Short History of Standing Armies in England* (London 1698)

Turner, Sir James, *Pallas Armata: Military Essays ...* (London 1683)

Walton, Clifford, *History of the British Standing Army 1660–1700* (London 1894)

Waugh, Norah, *The Cut of Men's Clothes 1600–1900* (London 1964)

Documents in the Public Record Office, London:

PRO 30/37 *Private Ordnance Records*

SP44 *State Paper Domestic*

WO4/1 *Secretary at War. Out Letter March 1684 to December 1690*

WO5/1 *Out Letters – Marching Orders 1683–85*

WO24 *Establishments 1661–1846*

WO26/1–6 *Miscellany Books*

WO47/1–19b *Board of Ordnance*

WO50/1 *Bill Books 1677–79*

WO55 *Warrants*

Documents in the British Library Manuscript Room:

Add. 10123 *Montagu Army Accounts 1680–1699*

Add. 10115 *Williamson Papers relating to the proposed French War of 1677*

Add. 15893/f.405 *Accounts of Major William Barker's Company 1686*

Add. 15897 *Winter Quarters of Forces 1686 and Abstract of Establishments*

Add. 23642 *Tyrawly Papers 1679–1759*

Add. 34516 *Makintosh Army Papers 1685–86*

Right: The battle of the Boyne. Most artillery remained too cumbersome to be moved during a battle; but, during the reign of James II mobile 3-pounder cannons were attached to foot regiments and were served by soldiers drawn from their ranks. Detail of The Battle of the Boyne, 1690 *by Jan Wyck. (National Army Museum)*

Table C: British Regiments at Tillroy Camp, 1689

From *A list of our Army as it was drawn up at Tillroy Camp, 1689* – this is an extract showing British regiments only.

Regiment	Clothing colour	Men	Notes
The Horse			
Duke of Ormond	Red lined blue	60	Horse Grenadiers
Duke of Ormond	Red lined blue	200	2nd Troop, Horse Guards
Oxford	White lined scarlet	400	Should be blue lined scarlet
The Foot			
Talmash Guards	Red lined white	1,000	Coldstream Guards
Part of the Scotch Guards	Red lined white	700	
Fuzileers	Red lined yellow	780	7th Foot
Hales	Red lined white	780	
O'Farrell Fuzileers	Red lined green	780	Raised 1688, disbanded 1699
FitzPatrick	Red lined green	780	Raised 1688 as Bevil Skelton's; disbanded 1701
Churchill	Red lined buff	780	Raised 1688 as Bevil Skelton's; disbanded 1701
Hodges	Red lined red	780	3rd Foot, Holland Regiment
Count Shamburg	Red lined white	780	16th Foot (white lining in 1691)
			Royal Scots

THE PLATES

A: The Restoration
A1: Trooper, The King's Troop of Horse Guards, 1661

The Horse Guards took a prominent part in the coronation of Charles II and were described by Sir Edmund Walker as 'The Kings Horse Guard, all well mounted, having Buffe Coates, with white Armour, their Horses furnished with Hooses (being a short Foot cloth) with red Scarfes, & plumes of Red & white feathers'. Eight years later the Horse Guards are recorded wearing red coats with blue facings. Hollar's engraving of the Horse Guards gives no indication of colours, though small figures in the background of an oil painting of the coronation confirm that buff coats were worn.

A2: Musketeer, Lord Wentworth's Foot Guards, 1662

In 1662 Dunkirk was sold to the French and Lord Wentworth's Regiment returned to England. The style of dress is French reflecting the regiment's re-equipment in Dunkirk. Although the knee-length coat had not yet appeared, the cassack had replaced the doublet for the French Guards. The matchlock musket was now used without a rest while the bandoleer of charges continued to contain the musketeer's gunpowder, and was not to be replaced completely by the cartridge box until after the end of the century.

A3: Pikeman, The Coldstream Regiment of Foot Guards, 1669

During his visit to England, Duke Cosmo noted that the pikemen of the Guards regiments wore reverse coat colours to musketeers. Pikemen had discarded their armour in the Civil Wars mainly because it was heavy on the march, and offered little protection against musketry. The more static duties of peacetime encouraged the reintroduction of armour, but by the late 1670s it disappeared once again.

B: The Regimental tailor at work, 1686
B1: Regimental tailor

The quality of uniforms was poor and only rarely was any attempt made to offer a choice of sizes. The regimental tailor had a great deal of work to do whenever new uniforms were issued, since the garments needed extensive adjustments before they would fit many individuals. The tailor wears a simple shirt made with no yoke over the

The main role of the pikeman was to protect the musketeer from cavalry, and when there was a threat to its flanks a unit would form a pike ring. English soldiers in Portugal in the 1660s fought off overwhelming numbers of Spanish cavalry by forming a pike and musket square. From The Wars of William III and Queen Anne *by Brig-Gen Kane, 1735. (Private Collection)*

HOLLOW-SQUARE ATTACK'D
By Horse on all Sides.

houlders. A simple strip of linen is worn as a cravat, protecting the neck from the rubbing of coat and waistcoat. The breeches are cut baggy as there was little stretch in the cloth used and when secured below the knee a tight pair of breeches could make bending the legs difficult, as when kneeling during volley firing.

B2: Soldier in sleeved waistcoat, Prince George of Denmark's Regiment of Foot

This soldier is undergoing the annual task of having his previous year's uniform coat converted into a waistcoat. His regiment wears a red coat lined yellow, and his old coat has been dismantled and the cloth turned inside out, so that his waistcoat will be yellow lined red. The cloth is relatively clean as the face, earlier protected between coat and lining, is now outermost.

B3: Officer, The Earl of Oxford's Horse

In 1686 the Earl of Oxford set down the first recorded uniform code for his officers: '*All the Captains coats are to e of blue cloth faced with the same, the lace of the said coats to e of gold, laid double upon every seam and slits with a gold oot between the two laces. The buttons of gold thread with a old fringe round the sleeves, under which must be laid the ame lace as down the seams. All the Lieutenant's and Cornet's coats must be the same as the Captain's, only a single road lace on each seam and slits and sleeves, the fringe xcepted. The Quartermaster's coats must be the same cloth as he rest of the Officer's with a gold edging down before, at the ockets, slits and round the sleeves, with a broad lace round the leeves, as the Lieutenants and Cornets, and gold buttons as he rest of the Officers. The pockets of all the coats must be of he same fashion, viz., with two long slits on each side. Each fficer must have a black hat edged with a gold lace and a white eather. The trimming of the hats must be yellow as also the ravat strings.*'

B4: Soldier in watch coat

The coat and waistcoat proved adequate for normal ervice, but guard duty at night or in bad weather required xtra clothing. 'Watch coats' were issued to men chosen for entry duty. Later experience of prolonged campaigning ed to the introduction of 'surtout' coats as general issue.

C: Tangier, 1669

C1: Officer of the Tangier Garrison

The officers in Hollar's 1669 paintings of Tangier all wear lothing and hats of a light grey material. A waistcoat, also ght grey, is secured with a cord rather than a sash. Coat leeves are short and decorated with coloured ribbons. Ribbons of the same colour appear at the shoulders of the oat, and on the garters and shoes.

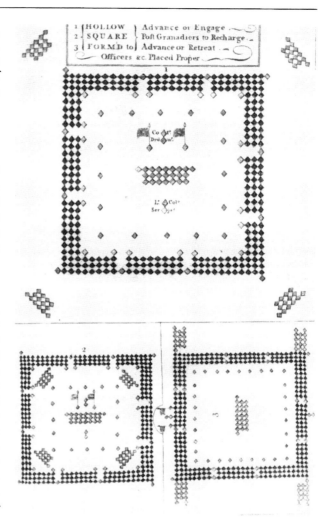

The infantry square was not a static formation. Here are diagrams for a battalion in square to advance to engage the enemy, to stand with its grenadiers withdrawn, and to march with 'wings' of grenadiers. From The Wars of William III and Queen Anne by Brig-Gen Kane, 1735. (Private Collection)

C2: Musketeer, the Governor's Regiment

A figure in Hollar's watercolours of Tangier, possibly a sergeant, appears in a grey coat; but the common soldiers all wear red coats, some with blue facings, breeches and stockings, and some with the same items in green. The musket was used without a rest and bandoleers were worn as crossbelts with a baldrick supporting a 'hanger' sword.

C3: Drummer, The Coldstream Guards, 1671

This drummer is based upon an illustration of the funeral of Monk which took place in the year after Hollar's visit to Tangier. Most companies had two drummers although the 'king's' companies of Wentworth's and Russell's Guards each had three. When, in 1665, these two regiments were merged they had one drum-major and 36 drummers between 24 companies.

D: The Virginia Expedition, 1677

In 1677 a composite regiment of 500 men drawn from the Foot Guards regiments, the Holland Regiment and the Lord Admiral's Regiment was dispatched to put down a rebellion in the Virginia colony. The regiment was reinforced by 630 'recruits', who may have been experienced men drawn from other regiments.

D1 Musketeer, The Lord Admiral's Maritime Regiment of Foot

This soldier wears the yellow coat of the Admiral's Regiment, and carries a flintlock musket which was standard issue for the regiment because of duties on board ships where the matchlock was impractical. He wears a waist sash of the type issued to new recruits in 1678 and shown in a painting of 1680.

D2: Pikeman, The Coldstream Regiment of Foot Guards

The 500 men sent on the Virginia Expedition who had been transferred from other regiments are said to have been armed in the usual ratio of one pike to two muskets. This figure is based upon a painting of 1680 showing the Coldstream Guards at Horse Guards Parade. His sword is supported on a baldrick rather than a waist belt, and unusually he wears no waist sash.

D3: Grenadier, Col. Herbert Jeffery's Regiment of Foot

This figure represents the 630 'recruits' who accompanied the Virginia Expedition and were placed in a composite regiment under Col. Herbert Jeffery. Each man was issued with a red cap, a large red coat lined with blue baize, a shirt, a coarse calico cravat, breeches, stockings and shoes. No pikes were issued, instead 300 matchlock and 200 flintlock muskets were provided, all with bandoleers. In addition 500 'cartouch boxes covered with leather, with girdles', 500 hatchets and 1500 hand grenades were also supplied. The fact that much of this was grenadier equipment suggests that the 'recruits' for the regiment were mainly veterans. Our reconstruction is based on the painting of grenadier Captain Francis Hawley, but with an earlier form of furred grenadier cap.

The disappearance of the pike led to a reconsideration of infantry tactics now that they were based entirely on firepower. This plate shows two formations for a battalion in three ranks: *(above) for the new shallower firing formation, and (below) drawn up six ranks deep. From* The Wars of William III and Queen Anne *by Brig-Gen Kane, 1735. (Private Collection)*

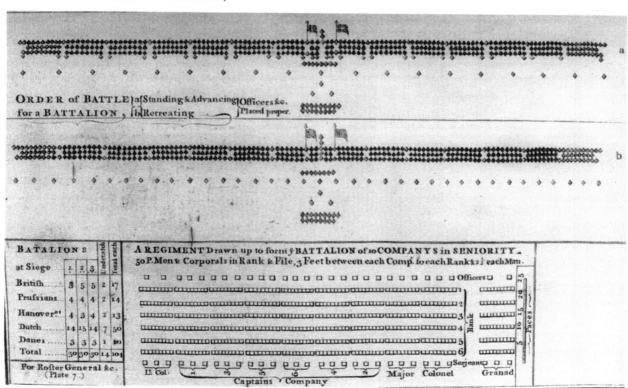

E: Sedgemoor, 1685
E1: Dragoon, The Royal Regiment of Dragoons

At the battle of Sedgemoor in 1685, the dragoons fought on foot on the flanks of the infantry battalions. The dragoon was not a 'skirmisher' in modern terms and in the open field fought in formed bodies, which drilled and manoeuvred in much the same way as infantry. At a review in 1684 the Royal Dragoons were 'Coated and cloaked red lined blue, housings embroidered with blue and yellow upon red, with the Royal cipher, holster caps the same, with the Royal Cipher'. Instructions from 1686/7 state: 'The Dragoons to have Snaphance Musquets, strapped, with bright barrels of 3 foot 8 inches long, cartouche boxes, bayonets, granade pouches, buckets, and hammer hatchets.' The dragoons of 1685 do not appear to have been equipped with grenades and it is unlikely that these were general issue.

E2: Field Officer

The dress of this officer is taken from the statue of Sir John Clobery in Winchester Cathedral. Clobery was colonel of a regiment raised during the time of Charles II and disbanded shortly afterwards. The monument dates from 1687 and shows the correct dress of that date. At the coronation in April 1685: *'The Officers of this First Regiment of Foot Guards were exceedingly richly habited; some in coats of cloth of gold, others in crimson velvet imbroidered or laced with gold or silver; but most of them in fine scarlet cloth, buttoned down the brest, and on the facings of the sleeves with silver plate. Their scarffs (which they wore about their wastes) were either network or gold or silver, or taffatta richly fringed with gold and silver, and their hats were adorned with tours of feathers.'*

E3: Piper, The Earl of Dumbarton's Regiment of Foot

As an 'English' regiment, Dumbarton's was forbidden to have pipers on its strength: bagpipes had been banned in Cromwell's time and anyone caught playing them was threatened with banishment to Barbados. In 1671 in his book *Pallas Armata*, Sir James Turner, who served in the Scottish Army, wrote 'any captain may keep a piper in his company and maintain him too for no pay is allowed him, ... the bagpipe is good enough musick for them who love it, but sure not so good as the Almain [i.e. German] Whistle.' A painting of the regiment at Tangier in 1683 shows pipers wearing the normal regimental uniform: red coats lined white, with grey breeches and stockings.

F: Horse Regiments at Sedgemoor, 1685
F1: Trooper, The First Troop of Horse Guards

When James II succeeded Charles II the troops of the

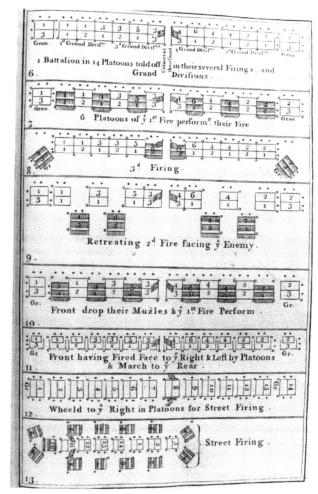

English drill had developed to encompass volley firing, but contact with the Dutch introduced the far more complex firing by sections. There is some discussion today about how often these forms of firing were used, and whether they could be sustained for long in battle conditions. From The Wars of William III and Queen Anne *by Brig-Gen Kane, 1735. (Private Collection)*

Horse Guards were numbered First, Second and Third. Sandford's *History of the Coronation of James II* gives the following description of the Horse Guards in April 1685: *'The Gentlemen of this Troop (200 in Number) were all new Clothed in Coats and Cloaks of Scarlet Cloth, lined with Blew Chalon: The Facings of their Sleeves, of the same Stuff, were laced about with a Figured Galoon of Silver (edged with Gold) two Inches broad: Their Buttons were of Silver Plate: They had each of them a good Buff Coat, and a large Pair of Gauntlet Gloves of the same: And in their Hats (which were Black, and turned up on one side, and edged about with a broad Silver lace) they wore large Blew Knots of broad Taffeta Ribband: which Blew being the Distinguishing Colour*

Four Dutch soldiers of William III's army. One has a soft, fur-trimmed cap, another a leather cap which may resemble those worn by English fusiliers. Plug bayonets and powder flasks are worn on a waistbelt. From left to right the uniforms are: (1) – black cap, red coat cuffs and stockings; (2) – grey coat and cuffs, red waistcoat and stockings, hat edged with white lace; (3) – red coat and cuffs with red waistcoat, grey stockings, hat bound with white lace; (4) – red cap edged with brown fur, red coat and cuffs, red waistcoat, grey stockings. All four figures have white metal buttons and buff leather equipment. The musket locks are difficult to identify, and have in any case been drawn incorrectly, fitted on the left-hand side. Pen and watercolour by an unknown artist. (The Royal Collection © 1993 Her Majesty The Queen)

of their Troop from the others, the Heads of their Horses were adorned with knots of the like Ribband. They were extraordinary well Mounted, and excellently well equipped, having their Housses and Holster-caps of Scarlet Cloth, Imbroidered with the King's Cipher and Crown within a Border of Foliage. Each of these Gentlemen was Armed and Accoutred with a good broad sword, and large Buff Shoulder-Belt, a Case of Pistols, a Carabine, with a carabine Belt of Blew Velvet 5 Inches broad, bordered with figur'd Silver Galoon, (edged with a narrow Gold Lace) in bredth 2 Inches, so that not above an Inch in bredth of the Velvet appeared.'

As for the officers of the King's Troop: 'The Officers of this Troop were richly Habited, either in Coats of Crimson Velvet Imbroidered with Gold and Silver, or of Fine Scarlet Cloth Imbroidered or laced with Gold or Silver, or both intermixed. They wore Scarfs about their Wastes, either of Gold or Silver Network, or Crimson Taffeta, richly Fringed with Gold or Silver on the edges, and with a deep Fringe of the same at the Ends. Their Cloaks were also of Fine Scarlet Cloth, Imbroidered on the Capes and down before with Gold or Silver, or both intermixed. In their Hats they wore Tours of White feathers; Their Housses and Holster-Caps being of Crimson Velvet, were richly Imbroidered and Embossed with Gold and Silver: And the Manes, Cruppers and Tayls of their Horses were garnished with large knots of Blew Taffeta Ribband.'

The Second Troop had fittings and ribbons of green; lace was gold edged silver, with the King's Cipher within a border of royal badges. The Third Troop had silver lace and yellow as its distinguishing colour.

F2: Trooper, The Earl of Oxford's Horse

The Earl of Oxford's Horse, also sometimes confusingly called the Horse Guards, wore the royal colours in reverse giving the famous blue coats lined red. This figure is based on a portrait of an officer of the regiment which shows troopers in the background; details are filled in from written descriptions. Grey hats were a distinction of this regiment, though pot helmets were probably worn in action.

COLLONELL

THE Lord Dartmouth's old Colours.

The Royall Regm.t of Fusaleirs have but three Colours of such kind of Trophee.

The colonel's colour of the Royal Regiment of Fuzileers. This and the following flags are taken from a book of pen and watercolour drawings which has been dated to c.1686. The colour illustrated is 'Collonel... The Lord Dartmouth's old Colours'; and so may no longer have been carried by 1686. It has a white background with a 'trophy' of standards and arms in gold. The stag's head was the armorial badge of the Earl of Dartmouth who was the regiment's colonel at this time. The lieutenant-colonel's colour is white, with a red cross of St. George, and with 'trophies' in the quarters; the major's is similar, with a red pile wavy in the first quarter. Another illustrated colour is similar to the lieutenant-colonel's, but with a cannon in the centre. From Drawings of Colours and Standards of the British Army. Tempore James II, Royal Library at Windsor Castle. (The Royal Collection ©1993 Her Majesty The Queen)

First captain's colour of the Holland Regiment. It is black with a red cross of St. George outlined in white, with a painted golden sun 'in splendour'. The roman numeral, in gold, denotes the seniority of the captain. The major's colour is as illustrated, but with a silver pile wavy replacing the numeral; the lieutenant-colonel's is as the first captain's, but without the numeral; and the colonel's is a plain black flag bearing only the gold sun in splendour device. (The Royal Collection ©1993 Her Majesty The Queen)

F3: Horse Grenadier, The First Troop of Horse Guards

Each troop of Horse Guards had an attachment of 60 'Horse Grenadiers'. Whereas Horse Guard troopers were gentlemen volunteers, these grenadiers were recruited men raised in the normal way by beat of the drum.

Sandford describes the first troop thus: *'The Granadiers (60 in Number) were Cloathed in Coats of Fine Red Cloth, Lined and Faced with Blew Chalon, and Buttoned with White Mettle hatched with Silver. On the Brest, Arms, and Facings of the Sleeves, they wore large Loops of Fine Blew*

First captain's colour of the Coldstream Guards. It has a white field with red or crimson cross of St. George, and crown and company numeral in gold. The colonel's colour is plain white with no devices, and the lieutenant-colonel's has only a red cross and a crown in the centre. The major's had the St. George's cross, with a central crown, and a pile wavy in the first quarter. (The Royal Collection ©1993 Her Majesty The Queen)

Lieutenant-colonel's colour of the Queen Consort's Regiment of Foot. It has the usual red cross of St. George on a plain white field, but each quarter is blazoned with five black eagles – the eagle was the family badge of Marie of Modena. The colonel's colour is white with the Queen Consort's entwined cipher 'MEBR' (Marie Eleanore Beatrice Regina) under a crown, both in gold. The remaining flags have the same red cross and five eagles in each quarter; the major's colour has a red pile wavy in the first canton, while the captain's colours have a crown and cipher. (The Royal Collection ©1993 Her Majesty The Queen)

Worsted, Edged and Tufted with Black and White. The Crowns of their Caps were raised high to a point, falling back at the top in Form of a Capouch, which were turned up before and behind, Triangular, and Faced with Blew Plush; and on the back of the Crowns was a Roundel or Granada-Ball also of the same. Their Cloaks were of Fine Red Cloth, Lined with Blew, and their Hats being Black, and Laced about with Silver, were buttoned up, and adorned with Knots of Blew Taffeta Ribband, as were the Heads of their Horses. Their Holster-caps and Housses (scallopt on the Edges) of Red Cloth, were Imbroidered with the Royal Cipher and crown, and bordered with Foliage; so that being annexed or depending upon His Majesties First Troop of Horse-Guards, this Troop was agreeable unto them in all their Colours. Each of these Granadiers was armed and Accoutred with a long Carbine strap'd, a good Sword, with a waste Buff Belt, a case of Pistols, cartouch-Box, Bucket, Bionet, and Granada-Pouch.'

The Horse Grenadiers of the second troop were similarly dressed with green as their distinguishing colour; coat loops were edged and tufted with black and white, and buttons were gilt; lace was gold; hats and horses were decorated with green ribbons. The third troop's grenadiers were distinguished with yellow; buttons were of white metal and lace was silver.

G: Campaigns in Ireland
G1: Musketeer, Lord Cutts' Regiment of Foot; King William's Army, 1691
The regiment commanded by Lord Cutts in 1691 had been formed in 1674 in the service of the Dutch and was disbanded in 1699 in the demobilisation that followed the end of the War of the Grand Alliance. The Irish Treasury Papers for 17 April 1691 record the issue of 'Red kersey and buff baize' cloth for coats, 'white woollen hose' and '300 gross [that is, 300 × 144] buttons'. The style of dress is based upon an illustration of Dutch infantry of 1689. The bandoleer, although still in general use, was being supplanted in some regiments by a cartridge box worn on a shoulder belt.

G2: Pikeman, The Earl of Bath's Regiment of Foot; King William's Army, 1691
The Earl of Bath's Regiment was unusual in 1685, it being the only foot regiment clothed in blue coats (lined red). In 1691, like many newer regiments, it converted from blue to red coats. By the early 1690s the pike was in decline, and the number of pikemen in a company was soon further reduced. However, in the campaigns in Ireland the pike proved its worth in defending the inexperienced English regiments from the crack Jacobite cavalry; meanwhile veteran Danish regiments with no pikes were roughly handled.

G3: Trooper, Galmoy's Regiment of Horse; King James's Army, 1691
The horse was the best part of the Jacobite army and saved the foot from destruction at the battle of the Boyne. By this time the dress and equipment of the horse had been standardised throughout western Europe with only pot helmets and back and breast plates distinguishing the different formations. This trooper of Galmoy's Regiment still wears a buffcoat under his uniform coat, though by this date many horse regiments had opted for cloth waistcoats.

Although in a book published in 1689, the soldiers depicted here are dressed in the style of the mid- to late 1660s. The pikemen in the background still wear helmets and full armour. The officers have short coat-sleeves reaching to the elbow, and except where constricted by the cuirass, wear their long, knee-length coats open. The central officer seems to have a short waistcoat under his coat. From Military Discipline or the Art of War *by J.S. (London 1689)*

H: Artillery
H1: Fuzileer, The Royal Regiment of Fuzileers
In 1685 Lord Dartmouth raised a regiment of fuzileers to serve as a guard for the artillery. Matchlock muskets with their smouldering lengths of match-cord were a hazard among the open powder casks of the artillery, and the new regiment was instead armed completely with flintlocks; these had straps so that they could be worn over the shoulder. The men were dressed in red coats lined yellow, with grey breeches and stockings. They were equipped with bayonets, and with cartridge boxes worn on waist girdles. One company was designated as the 'Myners company' and was given 'Byonetts Extraordnary' – possibly sword bayonets. The miners also received 'Copper Plates whereon are cast Trophies for Myners upon Cartouch Boxes'.

H2: Gunner, The Train of Artillery in Ireland, King William's Army, 1689
The gunners accompanying the train of artillery to Ireland in 1689 wore uniforms of a colour inspired by the recent triumph of William of Orange: 'Blue coats lined orange bayes with brass buttons and hats with orange silk

galoone'. This did not yet signal the adoption of blue as the distinguishing colour of the British artillery since many foot regiments also wore blue at this time; the gunners soon reverted to red coats.

H3: Gunner, The Train of Artillery in Flanders, 1695

This figure is based on a uniform issue recorded in the Ordnance Office 'Entry Book of Bills': '*1696, March 31st. For the service of ye Traine of Artillery in Flanders. For Gunners. Crimson cloth coats, lined with blue serge with a flapp on ye button hole side & flapp pocketts, ye sleev's faced with blue cloth with a gold edging round ye cuff & buttons of blue cloth topt with gold & ye button holes loopt with ye same ... 144. Blew cloth wastcoats lined, ye body & sleev's with garlix ye skirts & sleeve hands with blue Padua, flapp pocketts small brass buttons & silk holes ... 144. Blue cloth breeches to button at knees, lined with linen & leather pocketts*

brass buttons & holes of blue silk ... 144 pr. Blue worsted stockings for rowling ... 144 pr. Strong shoes of neats leather waxt ... 144 pr Black hatts edged with gold & hatbands ... 144. Gloves topt & lined ... 144 pr.'

H4: Pioneer, The Train of Artillery; King James's Army, 1688

Pioneers were essential in an army that hoped to move heavy siege guns: roads had to be widened or improved, and bridges constructed or strengthened. When the destination was reached, pioneers were needed to construct gun positions and to dig trenches. The new train of 1688 had its own pioneers dressed all in red. Later in the same year, probably when William of Orange took command, the pioneers were issued with a cap embroidered with a shovel, a blue coat lined orange, an orange waistcoat, and blue breeches and stockings.

the Irish Battery

Part of Tangier from aboue, without the Water-gate.

The Horsseate a sandewich Tower ... *The Head Court of Guard.*

W. Hollar delineavit ...

Left: Maj.Gen. Randolph Egerton, who commanded a regiment of horse during the Civil War and earned his reward after the Restoration when he became lieutenant of the King's Troop of Horse Guards. His coat is red, though not of official issue. Beneath it he wears a full buffcoat with gold decoration along its sleeves. The cavalrymen in the background wear back and breast plates over their buffcoats and are engaged in close combat with pistols rather than swords. Though one of them wears a helmet, most have wide-brimmed hats. Oil painting by Jan Wyck, 1672. (Private Collection)

Above: An engraved view of the Tangier colony made from watercolours painted by Hollar on a visit in 1669. The two officers wear knee-length coats over short waistcoats with baggy knee-length breeches. The original Hollar watercolours show officers wearing grey clothing unlike the red of common soldiers. It has been suggested that this was a light 'tropical' uniform. Though the cloth used may have been lighter in weight, the cut was much the same as that worn in England. From Divers prospects in and about Tangier, exactly delineated by W. Hollar, his Majesties designer, AD 1669. (The David Carter Collection)

INDEX

Figures in **bold** refer to illustrations

The Wool Towns and Villages

During medieval times many villages and towns in the south of the county became centres for the manufacture and export of woollen cloth which made this one of the wealthiest areas of England. Today the legacy of the wool trade is seen in the old world charm of Suffolk's picturesque towns and villages, many of which appear largely unchanged over more than 400 years.

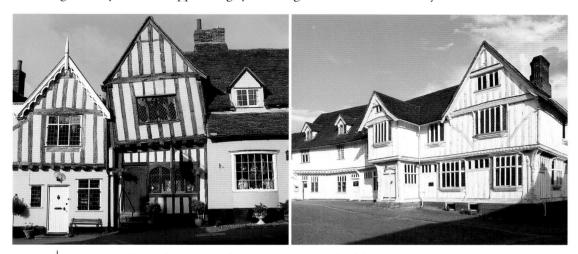

In **Lavenham** alone more than three hundred buildings have been listed as being of historical or architectural interest. Among this wealth of fine half-timbered buildings is the Crooked House, *above left,* in the High Street. Built in the 1460s it now houses an art gallery. Dominating the Market Place, the Guildhall, *above right,* is one of the best examples of Lavenham's many outstanding "black-and-white" buildings. It was built in the early 16th century and testifies to Lavenham's importance as a major centre of trade, famous for the manufacture of a woollen broadcloth known as "Lavenham Blue". The Hall has been put to many uses over the years but is now used as a community centre housing a unique exhibition of 700 years of the wool trade.

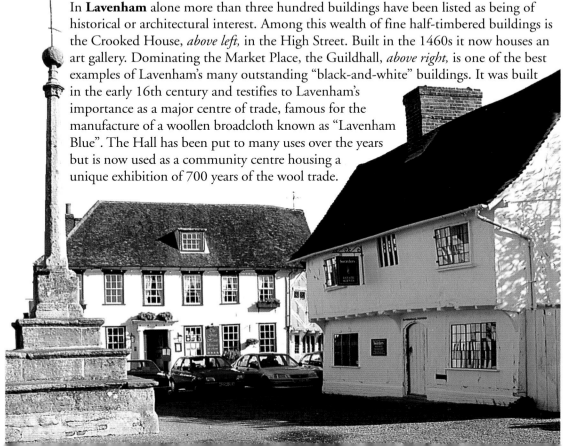

Not far from Hadleigh, beside the infant River Brett, lies the pleasant village of **Monks Eleigh**, *above,* where a number of old cottages stand beside the green in the shadow of the church tower. The village also has an attractive weather-boarded mill and the church is notable for its fine tower and carved pulpit. Home to a number of writers and artists in the first half of the 20th century, including Julian Tennyson, the great-grandson of the poet.

Chelsworth, *left,* is another charming little village which lies in the valley of the little River Brett. Handsome thatched, timbered-framed and colour-washed houses, most dating from the early 17th century, line the pretty main street not far from the river, which is spanned here by an unusual double hump-backed bridge.

Famous for the production of hard-wearing Kersey cloth, unspoiled **Kersey**, *right,* is one of the prettiest of Suffolk villages. Surrounded by the fields and hedgerows of this rural part of East Anglia, it is one of the most photographed villages in England. The magnificent Church of St. Mary stands on top of the hill which runs steeply down to a shallow water-splash. Medieval weavers' cottages are among the rich legacy of colour-washed and half-timbered houses, each one different from its neighbour, which line the curving main street.

Lying in the lovely River Stour valley, the village of **Cavendish**, *below,* boasts a number of charming thatched and colour-washed cottages which stand on the edge of the village green as they have done for more than 400 years. Beside them is the prominent landmark of St. Mary's Church which incorporates some fine Perpendicular work and has a distinctive tower topped by a pointed bell-cote.

Steeped in history, **Hadleigh** was one of the most prosperous towns in the country in the Middle Ages, and the imposing Church of St. Mary, *right,* stands at the heart of the medieval town. It is known for its fine east window and 14th century octagonal font. In the churchyard the site can be seen where, in 1555, the rector was burnt at the stake under the persecutions of Queen Mary. Next to the church is the red-brick Deanery Tower which was built in 1495, and nearby stands the fine timbered Guildhall.

Three miles north of Sudbury, **Long Melford** has a mile-long main street lined with pleasing frontages. One of the loveliest of the wool churches, 15th century Holy Trinity, *above*, has ninety-seven windows which give an impression of light and space. It commands the vast triangular green which is surrounded by elegant buildings from almost every century in the village's history. Here Queen Anne and Georgian buildings stand alongside fine 16th century timber-and-wattle houses.

Elizabethan **Melford Hall**, *right*, with its turreted gatehouse was built by a local lawyer, William Cordell, who became Speaker of the House of Commons and entertained Queen Elizabeth I at the Hall in 1578 during her Suffolk Progress. Before the estate passed into the hands of the Cordell family it belonged to the Abbots of Bury St, Edmunds. The bricks for the current house were made beside the village pond in an area still known as claypits.

An ancient market town on the River Stour, **Sudbury** was one of East Anglia's most important centres of the wool trade. It also acquired fame as "Eatanswill" when Charles Dickens wrote about it in *The Pickwick Papers*. Sudbury is perhaps best known as the birthplace in 1727 of the portrait and landscape painter Thomas Gainsborough, and the house in which he was born at 46 Sepulchre Street, *inset*, is now a museum and art gallery.

Clare retains many interesting old buildings including the remains of a Norman castle, which stands in a country park on the outskirts of the village, and the infirmary and church of an Augustinian priory which was founded in 1248. The centre of the village is dominated by the splendid flint-built parish church and the main street is lined with attractive houses. Many of them, like the Ancient House, *below,* which dates from 1473, display the fine decorative plasterwork which is typical of the county.

Ipswich and the River Orwell

Among many fine buildings in **Ipswich** is the highly decorated **Ancient House**, *below,* where it is said that King Charles II once hid. Also known as Sparrowe's House after the family that lived there for a long period, it was built in 1567. The main front is an outstanding example of pargeting, the art of carving plasterwork into decorative features and patterns. The panels under the oriel windows represent the continents of the world as they were then known.

The largest town in Suffolk, Ipswich stands at the head of the River Orwell estuary. A port since Roman times, it was an important centre for trading in wool, leather and fish, and was for centuries a thriving ship-building port. The docks extend for more than a mile along both banks of the River Orwell and the quayside, *left,* is still busy with both commercial shipping and pleasure craft.

The hamlet of **Pin Mill**, with its cluster of cottages and boat-builders' sheds, stands on the south shore of the River Orwell estuary not far from Ipswich, and is reached down a wooded lane from Chelmondiston village. A popular yachting centre, it is always crowded with boats of all kinds including some survivors of the old Thames sailing barges which can often be seen moored to the jetty. Overlooking the water is the Butt and Oyster, *right,* one of the finest of East Anglian pubs, equally accessible from land and sea since at high tides the water laps at its walls.

Situated on a gently curving bay between the estuaries of the rivers Deben and Orwell, **Felixstowe**, *left,* is a pleasant family resort with a two-mile-long beach backed by a wide promenade, lawns and splendid gardens which have earned it the title of the "garden resort" of the Suffolk coast. It was developed as a holiday destination in late Victorian times, and features such as the bathing huts along the promenade still reflect the atmosphere of a bygone age.

A wide, tidal river, the Orwell leaves Ipswich and flows through beautiful wooded countryside and parkland, passing riverside hamlets and ancient priories on its way to the coast. The marshes on either side of the river provide a welcome habitat for wild life and it is possible to see large numbers of birds, including migrants as well as native species such as cormorants. The river also offers delightful views of the Suffolk scenery and some fine coastal prospects as it enters the sea between the harbours of Felixstowe and Harwich. The magnificent **Orwell Bridge**, *right,* which spans the river just south of Ipswich, was completed in 1982. The main span of 190 metres was, at the time of its construction, the longest pre-stressed concrete span in use and is supported on pilings sunk 40 metres into the river bed.

The Suffolk Heritage Coast

The Suffolk Heritage Coast extends for fifty miles from Lowestoft to Felixstowe and is followed by a coastal path which offers superb views of the beaches, marshes, towns and villages of this evocative area. There are several long estuaries along this coast which ensure that the major roads pass well inland and so the coast preserves a sense of tranquillity. The winds and tides are constantly changing the shape of the coast which is famed for its quality of light, its wide skies and great cloudscapes. The area also attracts bird-watchers to the superb wetlands and salt marshes which fringe the coast. There are RSPB nature reserves at Aldeburgh, Orford, and Minsmere, where avocets, bitterns, and marsh harriers can be seen in addition to numerous butterflies and wildflowers.

A popular rendezvous for local yachting enthusiasts, **Woodbridge** stands on the River Deben. The picturesque white, weatherboarded Tide Mill, *above,* which was the last working mill of its kind in the country, was built in the 1790s and is the successor to a series of mills which have stood here since 1170. The silting up of the river halted the once flourishing ship-building industry, but the town still caters for yatchsmen with its modern marinas, chandlers and sail lofts. The fine Shire Hall, *left,* dates from Elizabethan times and was financed by Thomas Seckford, a considerable benefactor of the town.

Typical of the rural architecture of Suffolk, these fine 17th century cottages, *right,* with their thatched roofs and colourful cottage gardens stand in the village of **Ufford** near Woodbridge. The colour wash used on the walls, which occurs widely throughout the county, is known as "Suffolk Pink" and it is believed that it was originally made with a mixture of ox blood and whitewash.

Situated on the River Deben, **Ramsholt Quay**, *below,* with its waterfront pub, is a pretty little boating haven which attracts both local residents and visitors. The quayside, once busy with barges and other cargo boats, is now a favourite port of call for those enjoying boating activites of all kinds, and from the hill behind the tiny beach there are fine views of the river estuary.

Once an important medieval port but now a quiet riverside village where mellow old cottages surround the village pump, **Orford**, *left,* stands behind the ten-mile-long shingle bank known as Orford Ness. Built by Henry II in the 12th century as part of a network of coastal defences, Orford Castle commands a site overlooking Orford Ness and the surrounding countryside. The magnificent keep was the first in the country to be built to this design and its three massive battlemented towers remain almost intact.

Once it was an important east coast harbour, but today **Aldeburgh**, *above,* is a quiet resort with narrow lanes flanked by quaint old cottages, and a main street of elegant houses. The Moot Hall, *left,* a distinctive 16th century building of stone, timber and brick, was originally separated from the sea by three roads, since washed away in the process of coastal erosion. Today it stands in the middle of the seafront, where at one time an open market used to be held.

Snape Maltings, *right,* on the banks of the River Alde were used in Victorian times to process barley but were converted in 1970 to provide a concert hall for the famous Aldeburgh Festival which takes place each June. Attracting music-lovers from all over the world, the festival was founded in 1948, largely through the efforts of the composer Benjamin Britten and the singer Peter Pears. In addition to the concert hall, these remarkable buildings include shops, galleries and an activity centre, while outside the Maltings stand sculptures by Barbara Hepworth and Henry Moore.

The unique holiday village of **Thorpeness** was laid out in the early 1900s and has houses built in many different styles. It was planned around the Meare, *left,* an artificial lake used for fishing and boating, which is also a haven for wildfowl. One of its most unusual features, the House in the Clouds, *above,* was originally a water tower and water was pumped up to it by the splendid post mill which stands nearby. Built in 1803 the mill was moved to this site in the 1920s.

The magnificent ruins of **Leiston Abbey**, *right,* stand about two miles from the coast. It was originally founded in 1183 at nearby Minsmere, but in 1363 it was rebuilt on its present site. A substantial amount remains including parts of the transepts, presbytery and lady chapel. Inside the ruins there is a Georgian house which is now used for religious retreats.

First recorded in the Domesday Survey, the
little market town of **Saxmundham** has many
fine old buildings. These include ancient inns,
17th and 18th century cottages and an
impressive church as well as a sturdy Market
Hall, *above*, built in 1846 as a corn exchange.

Situated on a stretch of the Suffolk coast which has been at the mercy of the winds and tides
for many centuries, **Dunwich**, *below,* has been all but destroyed by storms and coastal
erosion. Once it was the seat of Saxon kings and a prosperous port, but today Dunwich
consists only of a few cottages and a shingle beach where fishermen draw up their boats.
Numerous churches and houses now lie beneath the sea and in 1739 the town centre finally
collapsed leaving only the ruins of a Franciscan friary still standing. It is said that when storms
are approaching the bells of the submerged church can be heard, ringing beneath the sea.

The peaceful little village of **Blythburgh** lies on the
River Blyth estuary just inland from the popular resort
of Southwold. The fifteenth century Church of the Holy
Trinity, *right,* is one of the finest of East Anglia's many
splendid churches and has become known as the
Cathedral of the Marshes. There are some unusual
carvings and marks on the pillars which are reputed to
have been left by Cromwell's troops.

Situated at the mouth of the River Blyth, **Southwold** is almost built on an island. To the north is Buss Creek, named after the herring "busses", fishing boats which were once a common sight on the waterway, and to the south by the river, which is lined at this point with boatyards and stalls where fresh fish is sold. Southwold's history as a fishing port goes back at least as far as the Domesday Book, but a shingle bar which built up across the harbour mouth prevented the town from becoming a major port. However, it remains a popular holiday resort and yachting centre and the river is always busy with colourful pleasure craft and fishing boats. Southwold owes much of its attraction to some imaginative planning after a disastrous fire destroyed a large part of the town in 1659. Among the open spaces created at that time is St. James's Green, *top,* surrounded by Georgian houses and overlooked by the fine white-walled lighthouse which was built in 1890.

A ferry, *above,* and a foot-bridge enable walkers and cyclists to cross the River Blyth from Southwold to **Walberswick**, an attractive village situated on the southern shore of the estuary. It is popular both with artists and with nature-lovers for here the Suffolk Nature Reserve includes some 1,000 acres of mud-flats, salt-marshes, heathland and woodland. Walberswick was once a thriving port, trading with countries as far away as Iceland. The river is quite narrow here and small landing stages run the whole length of it, providing convenient moorings for small boats.

Rural Suffolk

The pleasant market town of **Framlingham** is known principally for its Norman castle, *below.* Romantically situated overlooking the mere and the surrounding marshland, it has seen many historic events. Built for the 1st Earl of Norfolk on the site of a Saxon fortification, it was here that Mary Tudor was proclaimed Queen of England in 1553. The castle has been partially restored and the curtain wall and thirteen towers still stand with a walkway linking nine of them.

The village of **Laxfield**, *below,* near Framlingham, was the birthplace of the Puritan William Dowsing who, as Cromwell's agent, did much damage to the churches of Suffolk. The village boasts a fine restored Guildhall which dates from the 15th century and houses an interesting museum.

The post mill at **Saxtead Green**, *left,* is one of the finest windmills remaining in England. This was a thriving farming community in the 13th century and a mill was first recorded on this site in 1287. Still in working order, the present structure has been in existence since at least the late 18th century, but it was extended in the 1850s when two extra floors were added. It continued in commercial use producing flour until 1947.

Taking its name from the River Deben which rises here and flows alongside the main street, **Debenham** is a picturesque village and, despite a bad fire in 1744, many fine old buildings have survived. According to the Domesday Book, a church stood here at the time of the Norman Conquest and the present building incorporates some Saxon work.

Helmingham Hall, *right,* south of Debenham, is a moated mansion built in 1510 by the Tollemache family, Suffolk landowners since before the Norman Conquest and founders of the brewery which bears their name. Their descendants still live in the house which is surrounded by a 376 acre park with deer, rare breeds of cattle and sheep. The more formal gardens contain a parterre, a wild meadow garden and an outstanding Tudor-style kitchen garden.

Surrounded by delightful gardens, **Otley Hall**, *left,* stands half-way between Ipswich and Debenham. This outstanding 15th century timber-and-brick house is partly moated and is known for its superb panelling, its heavily beamed hall and for its Jacobean wall decorations. It stands in ten acres of formal and informal gardens which include nutteries, a rose garden and Tudor knot and herb gardens.

Agriculture and animal husbandry have been important industries in Suffolk since the time of the Romans, who were probably responsible for introducing cattle to the county. Suffolk cattle are valued equally for the production of milk and high quality beef, as are the popular Red Polls, *below,* which resulted from cross-breeding the Suffolk with the Norfolk breed at the beginning of the 19th century. The distinctive Suffolk sheep with their black faces, bare heads and bare, black legs are farmed extensively for their meat which is of a very high quality. A relatively large breed, they do not produce heavy fleeces. The oldest breed of heavy horse in the world, the Suffolk Punch, *above,* has its origins in the 15th century or earlier. Always chestnut in colour this magnificent animal stands about 16 hands high with a broad, deep body and short, unfeathered legs. It is known for its docile temperament which makes it particularly easy to handle whilst also possessing great strength.

South-west of Eye are the attractive little villages of Thornham Magna and Thornham Parva. St. Mary's Church at **Thornham Parva** is remarkable, although on a completely different scale from the one at Eye. This tiny thatched church, which stands beside an ancient trackway known as Grimsditch, dates from Saxon times. Among its treasures is an early 14th century altar-piece consisting of nine panels depicting eight saints and the Crucifixion. Painted in bright colours, the altar-piece was rediscovered in 1927 in the stables of Thornham Hall.

Eye is an ancient town, settled by the Romans and granted a charter by King John. The 15th century Church of St. Peter and St. Paul, *right,* has a magnificent 101 feet high tower and a striking rood-screen dating from 1480. Nearby stands the fine half-timbered Guildhall.

A few miles from Stowmarket is the ancient village of **Woolpit**, *left*. Although many Suffolk towns like Stowmarket grew and prospered on the wool trade, Woolpit is believed to take its name not from this but from a Saxon "wolf-pit" where captured wolves were thrown. An attractive 400-year-old coaching inn stands beside the green near the centre of the village which also has a wealth of medieval and Tudor buildings.

Lowestoft and Waveney

The River Waveney, which forms the boundary between Suffolk and Norfolk, flows into Oulton Broad at Lowestoft before turning northwards to reach the sea at Great Yarmouth. Britain's most easterly town, **Lowestoft**, *below,* has been an important port since the early years of the 19th century and there is still a flourishing fish market in the town. Today the harbour is busy with vessels serving the North Sea oil industry, while the yacht basin caters for small-boat enthusiasts. Lowestoft is also one of Suffolk's most popular resorts. It is divided into two parts by the estuary of the River Lothing, with sandy beaches to the south of the river, and the commercial centre and quaint old town to the north. The newer of Lowestoft's two piers, opened in 1903, Claremont Pier was built by a steamship company to provide a port of call for the passenger steamers which operated from London Bridge to the coastal resorts of Suffolk and Essex. The buildings at the shoreward end offer a range of leisure activities including a nightclub and a restaurant.

Fed by the River Waveney, **Oulton Broad**, *below*, is the most southerly of the Broads and is connected to Lowestoft by a lake. This popular yachting centre, with its moorings, boatyards and hire facilities, is always busy with pleasure craft, both motor and sail especially in the summer months when regattas and a water carnivals are added attractions.

The popular little holiday villages of **Corton**, *above*, and **Hopton-on-Sea**, with their safe bathing beaches, are backed by woodland and open countryside. Footpaths lead down through low, crumbling cliffs to the beach. The New Church of St. Margaret's at Hopton, *left,* was built in 1866 to replace the existing church which had been destroyed by fire in the previous year.

Situated just south of Lowestoft, **Kessingland** is a fishing village where the sea plays a very important part in village life. Even the lofty church tower, built in the 17th century, was used as a navigational aid for shipping. Here, in a former coastguard station, lived H. Rider Haggard, author of such famous works as *King Solomon's Mines* and *She*. Kessingland's beach consists of a wide shingle bank where boats are drawn up when they are not at sea.

Somerleyton Hall, an extravagant 19th century mansion which stands not far from Lowestoft, was built around the shell of an earlier Tudor and Jacobean house. The state rooms contain fine paintings and carvings and in the gardens, little changed since Victorian times, there are abundant flowering trees and shrubs, statuary and a remarkable maze.

The village of **St. Olaves** on the River Waveney is the site of an Augustinian priory which was founded in 1239. It was dedicated to Saint Olaf, the king of Norway who was responsible for bringing Christianity to Norway in the 11th century. Now ruined, a drainage windpump stands on the site. At its height, the priory was allowed to hold an annual fair on 29th July, St. Olaf's Day. The suspension bridge, *left*, which replaced the original ferry is the first bridging point on the River Waveney above Great Yarmouth.

Once a broad tidal estuary where wherries and barges traded, the River Waveney, *above,* is now used mainly by pleasure craft, and as the river widens out near the largely Georgian town of **Beccles**, provides good opportunities for sailing. St. Michael's Church, *right,* which dates from about 1370 stands in a commanding position overlooking the valley and from the churchyard there are delightful views of the river as it winds through the town and the surrounding countryside.

An ancient, and once affluent town, **Bungay** retains a number of fine old buildings. There has been a castle on this site since pre-Roman times, but the ruined twin towers and massive flint walls which still brood over the town date from the 13th century, *left.* Bungay's two churches are separated by the ruins of a Benedictine nunnery. St. Mary's Church, now largely redundant, dates from the 15th century and was badly damaged by a fire that ravaged much of the town in 1688. Norman Holy Trinity Church, with its unusual round tower, overlooks the Waveney Valley where European otters find sanctuary.

Bury St. Edmunds and Breckland

Once a place of pilgrimage, the ancient market town of **Bury St. Edmunds** has a long religious tradition and the abbey was at one time one of the greatest religious establishments in the country. A monastery was founded here by the Benedictines in AD 945 to house the shrine of the martyred King Edmund, and it was raised to the status of an abbey, *below,* by King Canute in 1032. Rebuilt after a fire in the 15th century, it was finally destroyed during Henry VIII's Dissolution of the Monasteries. The imposing St. Edmundsbury Cathedral, *right,* surrounded by colourful gardens, occupies the site of a Norman church. Built in the late 15th century, it was accorded cathedral status in 1914 and is Suffolk's only cathedral.

Three miles south-west of Bury St. Edmunds is **Ickworth**, *left,* family home since the 16th century of the Hervey family. The present impressive mansion dates from the 1790s and has two curved corridors connecting the central rotunda to the classical-style east and west wings. The house contains a magnificent collection of Georgian silver, furniture and paintings, including some by Titian, Gainsborough and Velázquez.

The main street in the delightful village of **Euston**, *right,* is lined with a rich variety of black-and-white timbered cottages, houses of flint and brick, tile and thatch. Euston Hall was built in the mid-17th century for the Duke of Grafton who also owned land in London which became the site of Euston Station, taking its name from the village. The Hall, which was largely rebuilt in the 20th century, contains some fine paintings, and in the grounds is the little Church of St. Genevieve. This exhibits some medieval work but dates mainly from the 1670s and contains exquisite carvings which have been attributed to Grinling Gibbons.

The **West Stow Anglo-Saxon Village**, *left*, is set in a 125 acre country park with a heathland nature reserve of woods, a river and a lake. Covered by sand since the 13th century, the site was excavated in the late 1960s which provided a unique opportunity to study an entire Anglo-Saxon village as it had been between the 5th and 7th centuries. At the end of the excavations the village was reconstructed using only the tools and techniques which were available to the Anglo-Saxons. The houses have been built complete with benches, beds and other fittings.

Newmarket has been associated with horse-racing since the time of King James I, and strings of horses exercising on the springy turf of Newmarket Heath are a familiar sight. The headquarters of the Jockey Club and the National Stud are based in the town where there is also a horse-racing museum, *left.*

Well known as an RAF and United States Air Force base, **Mildenhall** is an ancient town situated on the edge of the Fens. It has a number of fine buildings and the old town is still centred around the market place with its 16th century hexagonal cross, *centre,* and town pump. The early-English church retains many of its Norman features and has some spectacular carving in the rooves of the nave and aisles. The Mildenhall Treasure, a priceless horde of 4th century Roman silver which was found nearby in 1942, can now be seen in the British Museum.

In the heart of East Anglia, straddling the border between Norfolk and Suffolk, lies **Breckland**, *bottom,* an area which is unique in Britain because of its sandy soil and dry climate. In prehistoric times Breckland was densely settled and much of the original woodland was converted into vast heathlands. Numerous round barrows and other Bronze Age remains testify to the importance of the area at that time. In the Middle Ages the population declined and central Breckland was largely given over to sheep. The landscape is now dominated by Scots pine and other conifers which have been planted to help stabilise the light soils.